SARATOGA

MINUTE MAN

FORT STANWIX

USS CONSTITUTION

WORLD TRADE CENTER

PERRY'S VICTORY

GETTYSBURG

VALLEY FORGE

ANTIETAM

FORT McHENRY

FORT NECESSITY

MONOCACY

MANASSAS

KOREAN WAR VETERANS AND
VIETNAM VETERANS MEMORIALS

FREDERICKSBURG & SPOTSYLVANIA

RICHMOND

YORKTOWN

APPOMATTOX COURT HOUSE

PETERSBURG

GUILFORD COURTHOUSE

WILSON'S CREEK

FORT DONELSON

KINGS MOUNTAIN

PEA RIDGE

STONES RIVER

COWPENS

MOORES CREEK

WASHITA

SHILOH

CHICKAMAUGA & CHATTANOOGA

KENNESAW MOUNTAIN

FORT SUMTER

FORT PULASKI

VICKSBURG

ATLANTIC OCEAN

GULF OF MEXICO

PALO ALTO

AMERICA'S BATTLEGROUNDS:
WALK IN THE FOOTSTEPS OF AMERICA'S BRAVEST

AMERICA'S BATTLEGROUNDS

WALK IN THE FOOTSTEPS OF AMERICA'S BRAVEST
BY RICHARD SAUERS, Ph.D.

A READER'S DIGEST BOOK

This edition published by The Reader's Digest Association by arrangement with Tehabi Books

FOR TEHABI BOOKS

President and Publisher: Chris Capen	*Editor: Nancy Cash*
Senior Vice President: Sam Lewis	*Editor: Terry Spohn*
Director, Corporate Publishing: Chris Brimble	*Assistant Editor: Katie Franco*
Vice President and Creative Director: Karla Olson	*Copy Editor: Lisa Wolff*
Senior Art Director: John Baxter	*Proofreader: Jackie Garrett*
Art Director: Curt Boyer	*Indexer: Ken DellaPenta*
Production Artist: Mark Santos	

TEHABI BOOKS conceived, designed, and produced *America's Battlegrounds* and has developed and published many
award-winning books that are recognized for their strong literary and visual content.

FOR READER'S DIGEST

U.S. Project Editor: Robert L. Mills	*Associate Publisher, Trade Publishing: Christopher T. Reggio*
Project Designer: George McKeon	*Vice President & Publisher, Trade Publishing: Harold Clarke*
Executive Editor, Trade Publishing: Dolores York	

NOTE TO OUR READERS
The information in this book was gathered and carefully fact-checked by researchers and editors. Since
site information is always subject to change, you are urged to check the facts presented in this book before
visiting to avoid any inconvenience.

Address any comments about *America's Battlegrounds* to:
     The Reader's Digest Association, Inc.
     Adult Trade Publishing
     Reader's Digest Road
     Pleasantville, NY 10570-7000

For more Reader's Digest products and information,
visit our website:
     www.rd.com (in the United States)

Image credits appear on page 168

Printed by Toppan Printing Co. (HK), Ltd. in Hong Kong
10 9 8 7 6 5 4 3 2 1

The Library of Congress Cataloging-in-Publication Data

America's battlegrounds : walk in the footsteps of America's bravest.
     p. cm.
     Includes index.
     ISBN 0-7621-0582-8
     1. United States--History, Military. 2. United States--History, Local. 3.
Battlefields--United States. 4. War memorials--United States. 5. Historic sites--
United States. I. Reader's Digest Association.

E181.a455 2004
973--dc22

2004045351

"The time is now near at hand which must probably determine whether Americans are to be freemen or slaves; whether they are to have any property they can call their own; whether their houses and farms are to be pillaged and destroyed, and themselves consigned to a state of wretchedness from which no human efforts will deliver them. The fate of unborn millions will now depend on God, on the courage and conduct of this army. Our cruel and unrelenting enemy leaves us only the choice of brave resistance, or the most abject submission. We have, therefore, to resolve to conquer or die."

— *George Washington, 1776*

CONTENTS

INTRODUCTION

Benjamin Franklin once said that there was no such thing as a good war or a bad peace. But war has been almost a way of life for America. The United States was founded as a result of an armed revolution against Great Britain. A civil war in the 1860s held the nation together at a cost of over a million casualties. American involvement in two world wars spelled the difference between victory and defeat for the Western allies. Ever since World War II, American servicemen and women have served abroad, guardians of world peace and order in a world increasingly divided by religion, politics, and ethnicity.

The deeds and sacrifices of United States military personnel are highlighted by scores of preserved battlefields, ships, aircraft, military cemeteries, and other related sites and artifacts. Many of the most historically important sites are administered by the United States government's National Park Service, while other sites are maintained by state and local agencies as well as private initiative. This book presents to the reader a smorgasbord of battlefields and monuments that range from the Revolution to Vietnam. It's not a comprehensive survey; such a book would be a mammoth undertaking! But we hope that this collection of words, maps, and illustrations will propel you to learn more about the important role that war has played in American history, and how this nation has commemorated the sacrifices of patriots in defense of their ideals. All these sites are well worth a personal visit. They provide a stark reminder that freedom is not free.

Fort Sumter's garrison flag, below, flew during most of the bombardment until its pole was broken by a shell. A heroic Union sergeant nailed the flag to the shattered staff.

"The highest glory of the American Revolution was this: it connected in one indissoluble bond the principles of civil government with the principles of Christianity."

—*John Quincy Adams*

Reinforced by heavy cannons captured at Fort Ticonderoga, Washington's troops watched as the British evacuated Boston in March 1776. Four months later Congress declared that independence from England was its goal in the war.

The American Revolution started in 1775 and ended in 1783. Britain, one of the world's preeminent powers, was unsuited to fight a partisan war in which the Americans didn't conform to the European style of warfare. Incompetent leadership and bickering between generals paralyzed the English, who had to ship soldiers and supplies 3,000 miles across the Atlantic. Even though English victories at New York (August 1776), Philadelphia (September 1777), and Charleston, South Carolina (May 1780), meant that major cities along the East Coast were occupied by the British, they could never quite destroy the Continental Army, which, often outnumbered and always undersupplied, still managed to survive and confound the enemy. Washington may have lost more battles than he won, but by simply holding

The Boston Tea Party

his army together he also kept the dream of independence alive.

In the late summer of 1777, a major British offensive moved south from Canada, intent on splitting New England colonies from the others. American forces confronted the British advance and after a series of battles at Saratoga in September and October, General John Burgoyne surrendered the remnant of his army on October 13. The next year, 1778, saw France enter the war against the English. After a few years of military stalemate, American and French forces united to besiege Lord Cornwallis's army at Yorktown, Virginia. When Cornwallis surrendered on October 19, 1781, one of his bands played a tune entitled "The World Turned Upside Down" as the British stacked their muskets in surrender.

The Treaty of Paris was signed in September 1783. The American colonies became independent from England, but boundary questions remained to be resolved and the issue of debts owed to Britain by Americans and the status of loyalist property remained.

REVOLUTIONARY WAR WEAPONS

European armies of the late eighteenth century used smoothbore flintlock muskets, primarily with a .75 caliber, meaning that the barrel was three-quarters-of-an-inch in size. The British used a musket called the Brown Bess, the French used the Charleville, and the Americans used whatever they could find. Soldiers fought in compact masses that used speed to approach an enemy formation because muskets were rarely accurate at more than 80 yards. Aiming was not taught, only the volley-fire method by which a great number of guns were fired at a target; it was hoped some soldiers might get hit. When the enemy came within range, bayonets were used, although they were wielded more often as a psychological weapon than in actual combat. Americans used guns such as the Pennsylvania Rifle, so named because it had a rifled bore. A good marksman with such a weapon was deadly, as the British found out. But the rifle lacked a bayonet and could not be used in close combat. By the end of the war, the British Army had begun to form rifle companies to answer their opponents.

Guns were hauled by teams of oxen from Fort Ticonderoga for the siege of Boston in 1775.

FORT NECESSITY

BATTLE AT GREAT MEADOWS

French–English rivalry in the Ohio Valley led to armed clashes that escalated into open war in 1756. In 1754, English soldiers building a fort on the site of present-day Pittsburgh were driven off by the French, who erected Fort Duquesne. In April of that year, Lieutenant Colonel George Washington led a force of Virginia militia into southwestern Pennsylvania, tasked with building a road and assisting with the new fort. Once Washington learned of the French presence, he halted his men, waited for reinforcements, then pushed on to Great Meadows.

On May 28, 1754, receiving word that a small French force was nearby, Washington and a detachment of his command surprised the French camp and annihilated the enemy, but one man escaped to Fort Duquesne. Worried about French reaction, Washington's men erected a circular wooden palisade and dug trenches nearby.

A force of 600 French soldiers and 100 Indian allies arrived at Great Meadows on July 3. The enemy occupied the woods as rain began to fall, flooding the meadow and entrenchments. Washington's force of about 400 men remained in position and returned the fire of the French and Indians. Both sides suffered some loss, but at dusk the French sent in a flag of truce, requesting an English surrender. After some negotiations, Washington surrendered and was allowed to depart, his troops retaining their weapons and baggage. Once his men left on July 4, the French destroyed the fort and went back to their base.

The next year, 1755, General Edward Braddock led an expedition of 2,400 men toward Fort Duquesne. His men moved slowly, widening Washington's old road as they advanced, so the general divided his column and moved on ahead with half the troops. On July 9, when within eight miles of the French fort, Braddock's troops were ambushed by French and Indians. By the time the expedition retreated out of danger, Braddock had been mortally wounded and about two-thirds of his men killed or injured. Colonel Washington displayed great gallantry in rallying the troops and leading them in a retreat. Open war soon erupted between England and France.

Living historians demonstrate their skills.

French and Indians fire at Redcoats led by General Edward Braddock, who is seen falling mortally wounded from his horse. The mounted man at right is George Washington, who rallied the survivors and led a retreat.

"The rude bridge that arched the flood" over the Concord River is where Minutemen met the Redcoats on April 19, 1775. The famous statue of a Minute Man was erected here and stands guard to this day.

MINUTE MAN

THE SHOT HEARD 'ROUND THE WORLD

VISITOR INFORMATION

Name Minute Man

Classification National Historical Park

Established April 14, 1959; redesignated September 21, 1959. Boundary change: October 24, 1992

Contact 174 Liberty Street, Concord, MA 01742

Phone 978-369-6993

Website www.nps.gov/mima

Acreage 967.10 (Federal:790.29; Nonfederal: 176.81)

Points of Focus Battle Road Trail, Bloody Angle, Captain William Smith House, Daniel Chester French's Minute Man Statue, Fiske Hill, Harwell Tavern, Historic Farming Fields, Meriam's House, North Bridge, Paul Revere Capture Site

Tours/Paths Walking or bicycling on 5.5 miles of roads and wetland boardwalks, Wayside House tour, Life Along the Battle Road tour

Hours Open daily, morning until sundown. Closed Thanksgiving Day, December 25 and 26, and New Year's Day

Park Fee Free (fee for tours of the Wayside Home of Authors)

Programs 25-minute multimedia show at Minute Man Visitor Center, "The Two Revolutions" interpretive program. Note: Some programs are only available certain times of the year. Contact the park for specific dates.

Facilities Two visitor centers, gift store, museum, the Wayside Home of Authors

With Massachusetts declared to be in a state of rebellion, the English government appointed General Thomas Gage as governor. Headquartered in Boston, Gage tried hard to avoid inflaming popular sentiment against the Crown, but he was always on guard. On Sunday, February 26, 1775, Gage dispatched a force of soldiers to Salem to seize a cache of munitions said to be stored there; the British encountered hostile citizens and peacefully withdrew rather than continuing on their mission.

But two months later, the tense state of affairs between colonists and king erupted into armed rebellion. Gage had been ordered to seize rebel leaders such as John Hancock and Samuel Adams, but the general thought it more prudent to confiscate illegal arms and ammunition. Hearing of a sizeable stock of weapons in the town of Concord, about 20 miles west of Boston, Gage planned a surprise foray to capture the arms and return to Boston before word reached local militia units.

Lieutenant Colonel Francis Smith assembled a force of light infantry and grenadiers and had them rowed from Boston across to Charlestown early on April 19, then waited for supplies before beginning their march, hours behind schedule. By the time the British started their own march, Paul Revere and William Dawes, two members of the local vigilance committee, had raced ahead on horseback to spread the news that the British were coming. They were joined by Dr. Samuel Prescott, a Concord doctor who was returning home. British horsemen sent ahead to prevent just such warnings seized both Revere and Dawes, but Prescott got away and reached Concord to sound the alarm. Henry Wadsworth Longfellow's poem, "The Concord Hymn," penned decades later, made this trivial

The Battle of Concord Bridge with American Minutemen challenging British forces.

REVOLUTIONARY PROPAGANDA

The fighting at Lexington and Concord was barely over when the Massachusetts Provincial Congress took action. Postriders were sent out with brief dispatches to alert the other colonies. By early May, reports of the battles had reached Kentucky, where a party of hunters named their encampment Lexington to commemorate the rebels. A Boston newspaper, the *Massachusetts Spy*, had been moved to Worcester two days before the battle. The paper was soon churning out news of the fighting. Other papers followed suit and began preaching about the bloody butchery of the British troops. The Committee of Safety gathered depositions about what had happened and published *A Narrative of the Excursion and Ravages of the King's Troops*. Some of these depositions were sent by a fast-sailing ship to England, arriving ahead of General Gage's dispatches. Supporters of the colonial point of view had this material published and circulated around England to arouse support and question the use of troops against English citizens. Colonials thus garnered public opinion that helped their cause in the long run.

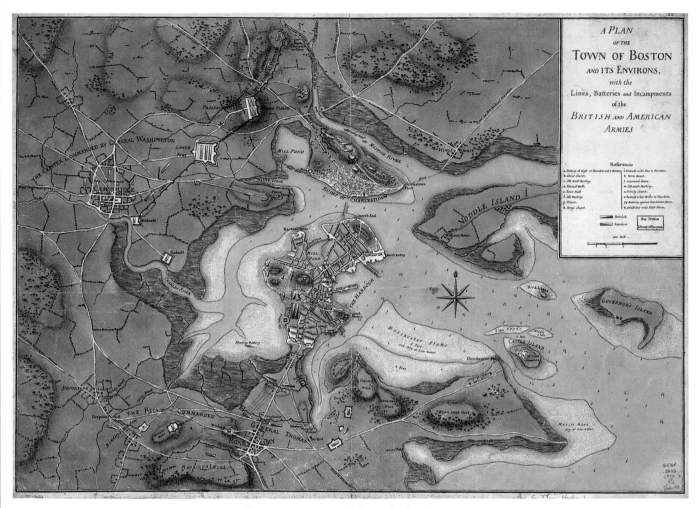

Boston, as it appeared during the Revolution

Front page of the Massachusetts Spy

incident famous and forced generations of suffering schoolchildren to memorize its epic lines.

By the time that Major John Pitcairn led the British advance guard into Lexington, local militia under command of Captain John Parker had assembled on the village green. Pitcairn called upon the militia to disperse and go home. As the Americans began to break up, Pitcairn's troops began to move in among them to collect their arms. A shot was fired, then others, and a British platoon fired a volley. When the major regained control of his men, eight Americans lay dead, ten others were wounded, and one Redcoat was wounded.

By the time the British reached Concord at eight o'clock, local militia had managed to remove most of the military stores, but the British began a thorough search of all structures in the town. Three companies went out to guard the North Bridge over the Concord River. When a sizeable contingent of local militia companies approached the span, the British withdrew, then fired a volley into the oncoming Americans, who returned the fire. But the Americans did not cross the bridge and the British finished their leisurely search of Concord, throwing whatever contraband they found into the local millpond.

At noon, Lieutenant Colonel Smith formed his men into column for the return march to Boston. He sent out flanking parties to protect the main force as it trudged along the dusty road. A low ridge to the north proved worrisome, but the British flankers kept the increasing number of militiamen at bay until the ridge ended a mile from Concord at a place called Merriam's Corner. Here the flankers joined the main column as it crossed a bridge over a small creek. This enabled Americans in the rear to crowd to the front and open fire on the Redcoats.

After crossing the creek, even though flanking parties managed to keep pursuing rebels far enough away, the British were subjected to a never-ending barrage of musketry. Colonials sniped at the distant troops from behind fencerows, trees, and buildings. Though the rebels caused relatively few casualties, the incessant rain of leaden musket balls unnerved the retreating enemy, which was unaccustomed to "skulking" warfare. Areas of the more intense fighting afterward became capitalized—Bloody Corner and The Bluff among them.

When tired British soldiers reached Lexington at 2:30 that afternoon, they met General Hugh Percy and his reinforcements of about a thousand men and two cannons. Percy allowed Smith's worn-out men to take the lead and then covered their retreat. He used his two artillery pieces with good effect, scattering large groupings of militia. Percy's flanking parties cleared

buildings along the road of their occupants, sometimes bayoneting those who resisted, always burning such structures to the ground.

Severe fighting took place at the small village of Menotomy, where historians believe about five thousand men all told were engaged in the shooting. Still, Percy kept his tired men moving to avoid giving the enemy stationary targets and thus prevented them from being annihilated by ever-increasing numbers of militiamen. By dusk, the British finally staggered into Charlestown, where they were protected by the guns of warships lying in the harbor. Wrote Lieutenant John Barker: "Thus for a few trifling stores the Grenadiers and Light Infantry had a march of about 50 miles (going and returning) through an enemy's country and in all human probability must every man have been cut off if the Brigade had not fortunately come to their assistance; for when the Brigade joined us there were very few men had any ammunition left, and so fatigued that we could not keep flanking parties out, so that we must soon have laid down our arms or been picked off by the Rebels at their pleasure."

British casualties totaled 273 killed, wounded, and missing, with at least 94 Americans slain and maimed. Armed rebellion was now the order of the day, and soon, General Gage was besieged in Boston. A severe engagement at Bunker Hill (actually fought on Breed's Hill) took place on June 17, but neither side held any advantage. At last, when the Americans received heavy cannons from Fort Ticonderoga, the British gave up and evacuated Boston.

British soldiers, marching back to Boston after destroying a weapon cache at Concord, are attacked by American militia.

THE AMERICAN REVOLUTION

MINUTE MAN

The term "Minute man" apparently was first used in Massachusetts about a year before the start of the Revolution. The provincial government disbanded all old militia organizations in order to purge Tories (loyalists) from the ranks. New regiments were created, with the officers being instructed to have a third of their men ready to assemble at a minute's notice. This one-third of each regiment was referred to afterward as "Minutemen." These units assembled at Lexington and Concord to oppose the British advance on April 19, 1775, even as the regular militia units assembled to fight later in the day. The Minutemen disappeared as an organization after the Continental Army was formed.

Minute Man Statue

VISITOR INFORMATION

Name Moores Creek

Classification National Battlefield

Established August 23, 1926. Transferred from War Department August 10, 1933; redesignated September 8, 1980. Boundary changes: September 27, 1944; October 6, 1974

Contact 40 Patriots Hall Drive, Currie, NC 28435

Phone 910-283-5591

Website www.nps.gov/mocr

Acreage 87.75 (all Federal)

Points of Focus Loyalist Monument, Moore Monument, Moores Creek Bridge, Patriot (Grady) Monument, Patriots Hall, Reconstructed Patriot Earthworks, Stage Road Monument, Women's Monument

Tours/Paths Self-guided Tarheel Trail, self-guided History Trail

Hours Open daily from 9:00 A.M. to 5:00 P.M. Closed December 25 and January 1

Park Fee Free

Programs Audiovisual tour in visitor center

Facilities Visitor center, sheltered picnic area

Bridge over Moores Creek

MOORES CREEK

AN ILL-JUDGED MOVEMENT

When the American Revolution began North Carolina was equally divided in sentiment. However, rebels forced Royal Governor Josiah Martin to flee from the provincial capital at New Bern to British ships offshore. Martin then organized a comeback by raising a loyalist army, supported by British warships, that sought to restore order in the province. By February 1776, Martin had gathered only about 1,600 soldiers, far short of his projected strength of 10,000.

The loyalists, under the command of British General Donald MacDonald, assembled at Fayetteville and planned to march along the Cape Fear River to the coast. A rebel force blocked their anticipated path, so

Women's Monument

MacDonald's column turned east toward another enemy force of militia protecting Wilmington. Though outmaneuvered by MacDonald's unexpected turn, the American militia hastily seized the bridge over swampy Moores Creek, 20 miles from Wilmington. Loyalists would have to cross the swampy region here, so Americans built earthworks and positioned weapons to cover the bridge, which was partially demolished to delay an attack.

MacDonald's men attacked on February 27. Their assault was met by a hail of gunfire and cannon shot as the American militia, led by colonels Alexander Lillington and Richard Caswell, mowed down the attackers. In only a few minutes, the loyalists retreated, having lost 30 killed and 40 wounded; only one rebel died. Although small, the fight at Moores Creek wrecked British plans for a quick, easy conquest of North Carolina.

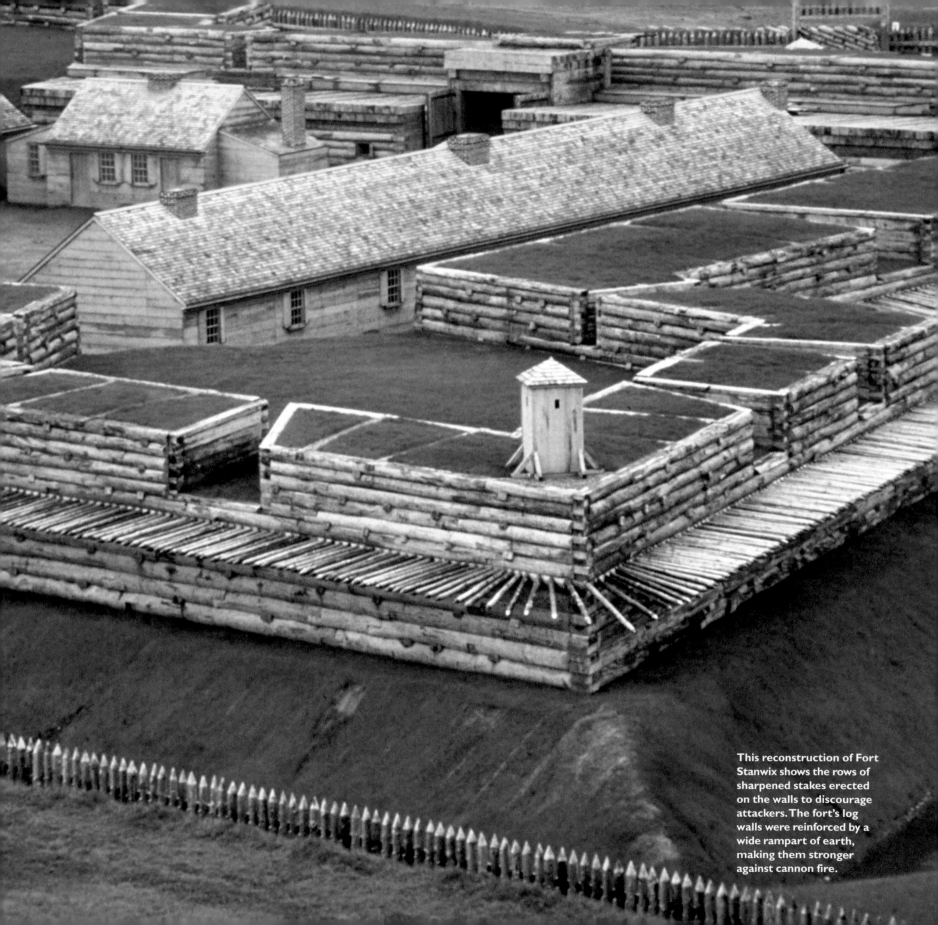

This reconstruction of Fort Stanwix shows the rows of sharpened stakes erected on the walls to discourage attackers. The fort's log walls were reinforced by a wide rampart of earth, making them stronger against cannon fire.

FORT STANWIX
TO THE LAST EXTREMITY

As part of the British strategy for the Campaign of 1777, a column of 1,700 British and Indians, under the command of General Barry St. Leger, was to advance east from Lake Ontario toward Albany, New York, supporting the southward advance of General John Burgoyne's army. St. Leger's column started its advance on July 26; by August 3, they had encircled Fort Stanwix, strategically situated at the junction of the Mohawk River and Wood Creek, at the present site of the city of Rome. Colonel Peter Gansevoort rejected St. Leger's surrender demand and a siege ensued.

Even though the British defeated an American militia force led by General Nicholas Hermiker at Oriskany on August 6, a sally party from the fort raided the British camp and carried off an assortment of supplies and trophies. General Benedict Arnold was then sent with a second relief column. Arnold enlisted the services of a half-mad local resident who had been captured while trying to recruit loyalists behind American lines; in return for clemency rather than death, this man (Hon Yost Schuyler) fled to St. Leger's camp with wild rumors about the size of Arnold's command. Schuyler pointed to the bullet holes through his coat as confirmation that he had escaped from the rebel camp (Arnold had ordered holes shot through the garment to lend credence to Schuyler's tale). Schuyler was followed into camp about an hour later by a warrior masquerading as a British sympathizer; this brave confirmed Schuyler's story.

As a result, St. Leger's native allies quickly melted away, refusing to fight the oncoming Americans. St. Leger then had no choice but to withdraw, which he did on August 22, leaving behind his artillery and camp equipment. Fort Stanwix played no further part in the Revolution; by 1830, the site of the fort had disappeared as Rome grew.

Fort Stanwix entrance

VISITOR INFORMATION

Name Fort Stanwix

Classification National Monument

Established August 21, 1935; acquisition completed 1973

Contact 112 E. Park Street, Rome, NY 13440-5816

Phone 315-336-2090

Website www.nps.gov/fost

Acreage 15.52 (all Federal)

Points of Focus Gregg Barracks, Living History Exhibit

Tours/Paths Three trails for self-guided tours

Hours Open daily from 9:00 A.M. to 5:00 P.M. Closed January 1 to March 31, Thanksgiving Day, and December 25

Park Fee Free

Programs Junior Ranger program, military drill demonstrations, Ranger-conducted interpretive programs, slide show, Summer Living History program

Facilities Visitor center, museum, store house

Barry St. Leger

VISITOR INFORMATION

Name Saratoga

Classification National Historical Park

Established October 15, 1924. Transferred from War Department August 10, 1933. Boundary change: January 12, 1938

Contact 648 Route 32, Stillwater, NY 12170

Phone 518-664-9821, ext. 224

Website www.nps.gov/sara

Acreage 3,392.42 (Federal: 2,884.88; Nonfederal: 507.54)

Points of Focus American River Fortifications, Balcarres Redoubt (Freeman Farm), Barber Wheatfield, Breymann Redoubt, Burgoyne's Headquarters, Chatfield Farm, Fraser Burial Site and Trail, Freeman Farm Overlook, The Great Redoubt, Neilson Farm (Bemis Heights), The Schuyler House

Tours/Paths 9-mile self-guided driving tour, 4.5-mile Wilkinson National Historic Trail, Guided Schuyler House tour; park open in the winter for snowshoeing and cross country skiing

Hours Visitor center: 9:00 A.M. to 5:00 P.M. all year. The Schuyler House and Saratoga Monument: 9:30 A.M. to 4:30 P.M. Wednesday through Sunday from May 25 through Labor Day

Park Fee $10 family annual pass; $3 for 7-day individual pass (for foot, bike, or horse entry); $5 for 7-day private vehicle pass

Programs 20-minute introductory film in visitor center, Junior Ranger program, Living History programs

Facilities Visitor center, picnic areas

SARATOGA
TURNING POINT OF THE REVOLUTION

British strategy for 1777 called for a three-pronged advance into New York, designed to cut off New England from the rest of the rebellious colonies. General John Burgoyne planned to lead an army south from Montreal. A second column would advance east from Lake Ontario, while part of the British army in New York would move north along the Hudson River. All three columns intended to meet in the Albany area, effectively severing American communications with New England.

Burgoyne's 9,000 men departed from Canada on June 17. By July 2, his troops had navigated Lake Champlain and had arrived at Fort Ticonderoga, which fell after a short four-day siege. As the British continued their southward march, American skirmishers delayed their progress, which was further hampered by rough terrain.

Saratoga reenactment

Unknown to Burgoyne, his expected help from New York would not arrive. General Sir William Howe was more interested in capturing Philadelphia, and that campaign was already underway when Burgoyne began his march. Howe's troops would not have time to return north to help Burgoyne.

The column under General Barry St. Leger also encountered difficulty. St. Leger's force moved into the Mohawk River Valley, then stopped to besiege American Fort Stanwix. Although his men repulsed a relief column on August 6, rumors of huge American reinforcements prompted St. Leger to fall back toward his base on Lake Ontario.

More important, a column composed of German mercenaries was detached to raid Vermont sites in search of supplies. American militia brought forces into combat at Bennington, Vermont, on August 16, inflicting almost 900 casualties on the defeated Germans.

Surrender of Burgoyne, October 17, 1777, painted in 1901 by artist Frederick Coffay Yohn, portrays Burgoyne offering his sword to General Horatio Gates, who allowed his defeated adversary to keep it. Later, Gates's surrender terms became a heated topic of discussion in the Continental Congress.

HESSIANS

This was a generic term applied to German mercenaries who fought for England during the American Revolution. A total of 29,875 Germans was supplied by six German states, with more than half coming from Hesse-Cassel and Hesse-Hanau, hence the term "Hessian." Although well-trained and equipped, German units themselves did not contribute significantly to British successes, but they were engaged in most major campaigns of the Revolution. When engaged by themselves against Americans, the Germans suffered defeats at Trenton, New Jersey, and Bennington, Vermont. Perhaps 5,000 of them deserted and remained in America after the war.

"Such an explosion of fire I never had any idea of before, and the heavy artillery joining in concert like great peals of thunder, assisted by the echoes of the woods, almost deafened us with the noise."

—Lieutenant William Digby, Shropshire Regiment (53rd Regiment of Foot)

Rather than retreat, Burgoyne doggedly pushed on. On September 13 he crossed to the west bank of the Hudson for the final leg of his march on Albany. But when his advance guard reached the imposing Bemis Heights, some 28 miles north of Albany, they saw American earthworks blocking the way. General Horatio Gates had just taken command of almost 9,000 American soldiers, which were well positioned to block a further British advance. Polish-born engineer Thaddeus Kosciuszko had laid out a system of entrenchments,

Surrender of Hessian troops at the Battle of Bennington; engraving by Alonzo Chapel

which commanded the river road below. Artillery was positioned to easily stop any British attack.

Burgoyne now faced a dilemma—retreat or attack. He chose the latter, still expecting Howe's troops from New York to come to his aid. On the morning of September 19, three columns of British soldiers left their camp and headed out on a reconnaissance of the American positions. American scouts soon spied the enemy and notified Gates, who sent Colonel Daniel Morgan's riflemen to confront the British. The two sides became engaged in the early afternoon in and around the farm fields of John Freeman, about a mile north of the American camps.

The resulting Battle of Freeman's Farm was a three-hour combat in which both generals fed in more troops. General Benedict Arnold's superb handling of his troops imperiled the British, but German troops from the River Road arrived to bolster the sagging British line and forced a reluctant American withdrawal, further hastened by a lack of ammunition. Although Burgoyne's troops held the field of battle, his men had suffered more casualties than the Americans—600 as opposed to 350.

Burgoyne then built two large earth and log redoubts to bolster the position at Freeman's Farm. The British then sat and waited for the arrival of help. As rations were reduced and the size of the American army grew as more militia poured into Gates's camps, Burgoyne finally decided on another advance against the American left flank.

The resulting October 7 battle was the pinnacle of the campaign. The British at first advanced more than a mile into cleared fields on the Barber farm, where Americans advanced at about three o'clock that afternoon. After an hour's savage fighting, the British line began to break under pressure from the

The Second Battle of Freeman's Farm was fought on October 7, 1777; when it was over, Burgoyne's army was finished, and with it British hopes for a quick end to the war. The wounded figure of Benedict Arnold dominates the center of this illustration of the American attack on the Breymann Redoubt.

numerically superior Americans. General Simon Fraser, in charge of the British right, was mortally wounded as he rallied his men to stand fast. At an opportune moment, General Arnold, who had been relieved of command by a quarrelsome Gates, rode into the field and led an American brigade in a charge against the German troops holding the British center.

The British line gave way and they fell back into entrenchments at Freeman's Farm. Here Arnold at first led an unsuccessful charge on the Balcarres Redoubt, then heroically led a surging American column against the Breymann Redoubt, one that overwhelmed its defenders. Arnold fell wounded in the leg as he entered the enemy earthwork. A later monument erected to Arnold's bravery depicts only a bas-relief of a boot without any written comment; Arnold's later treachery deprived him of a more elegant memorial.

Having lost eight cannons and more than 400 men, Burgoyne withdrew his army into the Great Redoubt, situated on high ground along the Hudson overlooking his camps. The next evening, the British began a 6-mile northward withdrawal to a fortified camp on the heights of Saratoga. Then followed a week-long ordeal never to be forgotten by those who survived. American troops surrounded the British and continually sniped at exposed men and lobbed artillery shells into the camp. Soldiers were forced to sleep on the cold ground, moistened by intermittent rain. Rations were in short supply and water came from a muddy spring. Wolves prowled among newly dug graves for the dead, and the camp followers, officers' wives, and other noncombatants were forced to share in the army's privations.

General Gates opened negotiations with Burgoyne, who on October 17 signed the Convention of Saratoga. By the terms of this treaty, Burgoyne surrendered his entire army of some 6,000 men, on the condition that it depart for England and serve no more in North America. But the Continental Congress mistrusted the British and served notice to Gates that the surrendered soldiers would be held as captives until the end of the war, lest the British use the freed soldiers as garrison troops in order to release other units for active service. Many British soldiers chose to desert during the period of their captivity, enticed by the promise of a better life in America.

Burgoyne's surrender at Saratoga was a major defeat for the British. The American victory helped pave the way for the 1778 alliance with France, as it entered the war against the British.

BENEDICT ARNOLD

Born in Connecticut, Arnold operated a book and drugstore prior to the Revolution. Arnold assisted in the 1775 capture of Fort Ticonderoga and was one of the main commanders in the failed 1775 American attack on Canada. Although defeated at Lake Champlain in 1776, Arnold's ragtag fleet delayed a British attack that year. In 1777, against George Washington's wishes, Arnold was passed over for promotion. His brilliance in relieving Fort Stanwix and his outstanding performance at Saratoga led to his promotion to command at Philadelphia, where he married the daughter of a loyalist family. Petty differences with other officers led to a court-martial, but he was acquitted. Thereafter, Arnold communicated with the British and planned to betray the fort at West Point to the enemy. The plan was revealed and British Major John Andre was captured as a spy and hanged. Arnold fled to the British, was given a general's commission, and led British forces in action in New England and Virginia. He moved to England after the war and died there in 1801.

Benedict Arnold

Reenactors on duty where cannons mark the site of the American artillery park. Brigadier General Henry Knox, Washington's artillery commander, collected all his cannons at this point. Here guns were repaired and crews drilled. If the British attacked, Knox could dispatch guns to critical points.

VALLEY FORGE

THE MAKING OF AN ARMY

Following the British capture of Philadelphia in September 1777 General George Washington withdrew his army and looked for a place to encamp for the upcoming winter. He selected Valley Forge, 18 miles northwest of Philadelphia, close enough to deter British forays into the countryside yet far enough from the city to prevent surprise attacks from the Redcoats.

Washington's 12,000 soldiers reached the area on December 19 and began building log huts to protect themselves from the cold. Soldiers erected more than 2,000 such huts during the course of their stay. But the shortage of food and adequate clothing was worse than the cold. Many dispirited and hungry men resorted to tasteless "firecakes," a concoction made from flour and water.

Washington himself despaired that the army might melt away unless Congress provided some assistance. During that winter of 1777–78, more than 2,000 soldiers died of disease. The quartermaster department was badly run and subject to graft and corruption. Congress failed miserably to come up with better controls and was unable to persuade the individual states to send more help. The continuing decline of the value of Continental money was always a source of despair.

To provide better discipline and training, Washington used the Prussian soldier of fortune Baron Friedrich von Steuben, who had served in the army of Frederick the Great. Working with American officers over the winter, von Steuben

Baron von Steuben

turned Washington's men into a better-drilled and disciplined fighting force. He first created a model infantry company, trained and drilled to perfection, that brought on a spirit of emulation for the other troops in camp. Speaking little English himself, von Steuben nonetheless drew up a drill manual in French, which his aides translated into English.

In March 1778, Washington transferred General Nathanael Greene to the quartermaster department. This dependable Rhode Islander soon transformed the department and made it much more efficient. New troops arrived in late winter, as well as more supplies. By the time the army broke camp on June 19, it was a far better organization than had endured the cold, hard winter at Valley Forge.

General George Washington

VISITOR INFORMATION

Name Kings Mountain

Classification National Military Park

Established March 3, 1931. Transferred from War Department August 10, 1933. Boundary change: June 23, 1959

Contact 2625 Park Road, Blacksburg, SC 29702

Phone 864-936-7921

Website www.nps.gov/kimo

Acreage 3,945.19 (all Federal)

Points of Focus Battlefield Trail, Centennial Monument, Chronicle Markers, Ferguson's Grave, Hoover Monument, U.S. Monument

Tours/Paths 16 miles of hiking trails, 16 miles of horse trails, 1.5-mile self-guided battlefield trail

Hours Open daily 9:00 A.M. to 5:00 P.M.; open weekends Memorial Day to Labor Day 9:00 A.M. to 6:00 P.M. Closed Thanksgiving Day, December 25, and January 1

Park Fee Free

Programs 27-minute orientation film

Facilities Visitor center, museum exhibits, campsite

KINGS MOUNTAIN

SHOUT LIKE HELL AND FIGHT THE DEVILS

After more than two years of inconclusive warfare in the northern colonies, the British shifted strategy for 1780 to the south—the Carolinas and Georgia. British commanders had heard reports that the Carolina back country teemed with loyalists, waiting for help from His Majesty's troops. A major British force captured Charleston, South Carolina, in May 1780; on August 16, the Continental Southern Army under General Horatio Gates was badly mauled at Camden, South Carolina.

Lord Cornwallis, in command of the British Army, decided to advance into North Carolina. Major Patrick Ferguson, a Scottish officer who had designed a breech-loading flintlock musket, had raised and trained more than a thousand loyalist troops to support Cornwallis's British Regulars. As Cornwallis moved north in September, he sent Major Ferguson into the Carolina back country with orders to pacify the region before joining the main column.

But Ferguson's high-handed actions only served to enrage men who already were loath to take orders. Four militia colonels gathered together a considerable force of men from west of the Appalachians and began crossing the mountains on September 27. Reinforced by local militia, the frontiersmen caught up with Ferguson's retreating force of 1,000 loyalists and 100 red-coated Provincials at Kings Mountain. This mountain was a natural fortress, rising 150 feet above the surrounding wilderness. From the summit, the defenders had a clear field of fire at any attacking force daring to brave the forested ravines between the mountain's flanks.

Led by Colonel William Campbell, the frontiersmen attacked on the afternoon of October 7. Twice repulsed at bayonet point, the Americans finally reached the summit and drove the enemy northeast along the crest. Ferguson was killed and his command annihilated; his men were either slain or captured. Upon hearing of the debacle, Cornwallis halted his planned northward march and went into winter quarters. The American victory at Kings Mountain had dealt the British a staggering blow that wrecked British plans in the Carolinas.

British forces surrender at Kings Mountain.

The Death of Major Ferguson at Kings Mountain. The major was hit by several bullets at once as he rode back and forth encouraging his men. He died shortly thereafter, propped against a tree. Ferguson's death discouraged his men, who soon surrendered.

The Battle of Cowpens, depicting the duel between Colonels Washington and Tarleton, painted by noted artist Alonzo Chapel in 1857. Washington's sword broke during the attack, but he was able to parry Tarleton's thrusts until two men rode to his assistance and the British retreated.

COWPENS

A BATTLE THAT "SPIRITED UP THE PEOPLE"

VISITOR INFORMATION

Name Cowpens

Classification National Battlefield

Established March 4, 1929. Transferred from War Department August 10, 1933; redesignated April 11, 1972. Boundary changes: July 18, 1958; April 11, 1972

Contact P.O. Box 308, Chesnee, SC 29323

Phone 864-461-2828

Website www.nps.gov/cowp

Acreage 841.56 (Federal: 790.90; Nonfederal: 50.66)

Points of Focus Robert Scrugg's House, Washington Light Infantry Monument, U.S. Monument

Tours/Paths 1.25-mile self-guided Battlefield Trail walking tour, 3.8-mile driving tour

Hours Open daily from 9:00 A.M. to 5:00 P.M., Closed Thanksgiving Day, December 25, and January 1

Park Fee Free; film admission: $1 for adults, $.50 for children ages 6–12

Programs 13-minute fiber-optic map program, 18-minute laser-disk film on the battle, Junior Ranger program

Facilities Visitor center, museum, picnic area

THE AMERICAN REVOLUTION

In 1780, General Nathanael Greene was sent to rebuild the shattered Continental Army in the Carolinas. To make it easier to both supply his own forces and confuse the British, Greene divided his army. He sent General Daniel Morgan into western South Carolina with orders to threaten the British left flank and rear. Morgan, a tough 45-year-old Virginia veteran, had played a key role in the victory at Saratoga, and despite suffering from acute rheumatism, had just rejoined the army.

Lord Cornwallis sent the brash 26-year-old Banastre Tarleton to chase down and destroy Morgan's 600 men. Tarleton had thus far served with distinction as a cavalry officer. Nicknamed "Bloody Tarleton," he had earned American hatred after his troops butchered surrendered prisoners in May 1780. Tarleton took command of 1,200 men and immediately pursued Morgan. After calling in local militia to help his veterans, Morgan deployed his men at the Cowpens, a frontier pasturing ground. Morgan's first line of sharpshooters was tasked with slowing the British advance before falling back. Militia in the second line had orders to fire two volleys and

Banastre Tarleton

then retire. Behind the militia were Morgan's Maryland and Delaware Continentals, together with veteran Virginia militia. Lieutenant Colonel William Washington, George's distant cousin, led Morgan's 125 cavalrymen, stationed behind the Continentals as a reserve.

Tarleton's advance guard reached Cowpens just before dawn on January 17, 1781. His cavalry drove into Morgan's first line as the British infantry deployed into battle array. As advancing Redcoats came within range, the militia fired two volleys and fell back as Tarleton's cavalry charged, only to be met head-on by Washington's horsemen.

The British then encountered Colonel John Howard's Continentals. Hand-to-hand combat ensued between the opposing infantry units. Howard began to pull his men back when outflanked, but Morgan rallied the army and attacked as Washington's horsemen again charged. Exposed to fire from both front and flanks, British resistance collapsed. Tarleton avoided capture, but more than 990 of his men were casualties, including 600 prisoners. The American loss was 128. As Morgan later said to a friend, his troops had given the British a "devil of a whipping."

Government Monument, erected in 1932

VISITOR INFORMATION

Name Guilford Courthouse

Classification National Military Park

Established March 2, 1917. Transferred from War Department August 10, 1933

Contact 2331 New Garden Road, Greensboro, NC 27410

Phone 336-288-1776

Website www.nps.gov/guco

Acreage 220.25 (all Federal)

Points of Focus American First Line, Cavalry Monument, Green Monument, Guilford Courthouse, New Garden Road, Signer's Monument, Tannenbaum Historic Park

Tours/Paths 2.25-mile driving tour, walking trails

Hours Open daily, 8:30 A.M. to 5:00 P.M. Closed Thanksgiving Day, December 25, and January 1

Park Fee Free

Programs 30-minute film, 10-minute battle map program, Junior Ranger program

Facilities Visitor center, bookstore, museum

Nathanael Greene

GUILFORD COURTHOUSE

A PYRRHIC VICTORY

Lord Cornwallis began his invasion of North Carolina in January 1781. General Nathanael Greene, outnumbered, withdrew ahead of the advancing British. After a three-week chase, Cornwallis arrived at the swollen and unfordable Dan River, facing Americans on the other side. Having expended resources to catch up with Greene, Cornwallis was now 230 miles from his base with his army worn out. He turned back, cautiously followed by Greene. After being reinforced, Greene moved closer to Cornwallis to goad him into a fight. Greene deployed his men near Guilford Courthouse, 12 miles north of Greensboro. He drew up his men in three lines and waited for Cornwallis, who attacked on the afternoon of March 15.

Greene's North Carolina militia held the first line, and staggered the approaching British with a well-aimed volley, but the Redcoats returned the fire and rushed in with bayonets, breaking the American front line.

The Virginia militia in the second line were posted on the edge of a wood and managed to delay the

Reenactors near the Cavalry Monument

British attack. Still, the British drove aside the Virginians and emerged into open fields, where Greene's Continental regiments waited. The advancing British Guards overawed the 2nd Maryland, which withdrew. Lieutenant Colonel William Washington's horsemen then charged, slashing at the red-coated infantry with heavy sabers. Greene's 1st Maryland Continentals stalemated the British Guards in fierce hand-to-hand combat around two American cannons. To break the deadlock, Cornwallis ordered his artillery to fire grapeshot into the melee, thus causing losses on both sides.

Greene then ordered a withdrawal. Cornwallis, left in possession of the field, had won a victory, but at heavy cost—93 killed, 413 wounded, and 26 missing, representing 27 percent of his 1,924 engaged strength. Greene's army lost all four of its cannons, and of about 4,400 soldiers, 79 were killed and 185 wounded. Another thousand were missing, generally militia who fled and failed to report back after the battle. The British soon began to march toward Wilmington to resupply, then turned north into Virginia, where Cornwallis had a date with destiny at Yorktown.

Lieutenant Colonel Henry "Lighthorse Harry" Lee, commanding his American cavalry, is depicted in skirmish with the advancing British. Lee's horsemen engaged the enemy for 5 miles before the two armies confronted each other at Guilford Courthouse.

Fierce hand-to-hand fighting took place during the capture of British positions that became American siege trenches, as portrayed here in *Capture of Yorktown*, a lithograph by Turgis.

YORKTOWN

THE WORLD TURNED UPSIDE DOWN

VISITOR INFORMATION

Name Yorktown

Classification National Historical Park

Established Park—July 3, 1930; redesignated June 5, 1936. Boundary changes: August 22, 1933; June 5, 1936; June 15, 1938; December 24, 1942; April 22, 1944; December 23, 1944; May 12, 1948; September 23, 1950; May 13, 1953; March 29, 1956; August 29, 1967. Cemetery—Date of Civil War interments: 1866. Transferred from War Department August 10, 1933

Contact P.O. Box 210, Yorktown, VA 23690

Phone 757-898-3400

Website www.nps.gov/colo

Acreage Park— 9,349.28 (Federal: 9,271.30; Nonfederal: 77.98). Cemetery—2.91 (all Federal)

Points of Focus General Washington's Headquarters, Historic Yorktown, Jamestown Island, Moore House, Surrender Field, Victory Monument, Yorktown National Cemetery

Tours/Paths Battlefield self-guided driving tour, Allied Encampment self-guided driving tour, two Ranger-guided walking tours, various hiking and biking trails

Hours Visitor center open daily from 9:00 A.M. to 5:00 P.M. Closed December 25 and January 1

Park Fee $5 for adults 17 and older; Yorktown/ Jamestown combination park ticket $9

Programs 15-minute orientation film, artillery demonstration, Colonial Junior Ranger program, interpretive programs

Facilities Visitor center, observation deck, museum, bookstore, picnic area

After retreating from Guilford Courthouse to Wilmington, North Carolina, General Cornwallis decided to abandon the Carolinas and move into Virginia, against the wishes of the British commander in North America, Henry Clinton. Cornwallis arrived at Petersburg, Virginia, in late May 1781, where he took command of 7,200 British troops. Governor Thomas Jefferson, himself forced to flee Charlottesville when an enemy raiding party routed the Colonial Assembly there, helped materially in gathering militia and supplies, but the British generally were able to go where they wished.

In early July, Cornwallis established a base at Yorktown, located on the York River down the peninsula from Williamsburg, which he fortified with earthworks and cannons. While the British generals argued over strategy via letter with the government in London, George Washington saw an opportunity to inflict a major defeat on the enemy. French infantry were already present with Washington's army near New York, but word of the imminent arrival of a large French fleet under Admiral Comte de Grasse meant the

Lord Cornwallis

allies might have temporary naval superiority and entrap Cornwallis.

Washington and the French general Comte de Rochambeau marched south to Chesapeake Bay where they boarded transports and landed in Virginia on September 18. The French fleet was reinforced by a second squadron that slipped away from its British counterpart and brought Rochambeau's heavy artillery. As the allies assembled, the Marquis de Lafayette, in command of allied troops watching Cornwallis, was tasked with preventing Cornwallis from leaving Yorktown before the allied vise was in place.

By the time Cornwallis realized his predicament, more than 17,000 American and French troops, supported by the French siege train, surrounded Yorktown and prevented Cornwallis from escaping. The general's only hope was support from the Royal Navy. Admiral Thomas Graves's squadron of 19 ships sailed south from New York to counter de Grasse's ships before he was reinforced by a squadron sailing from Newport, Rhode Island. Normally aggressive, the British in this instance proved to be sluggish. After several days of

An idealized and historically inaccurate portrait of Lord Cornwallis (Charles Cornwallis, later 1st Marquis Cornwallis) handing over his sword in a gesture of surrender to George Washington after his defeat at Yorktown, Virginia. In reality Cornwallis's second in command, Major General Charles O'Hara, surrendered his sword to Washington's second in command, Major General Benjamin Lincoln.

maneuvering and skirmishing, neither fleet was able to secure advantage, and the British, after the French were reinforced to 36 warships, sailed back to New York.

This lackluster British naval performance sealed Cornwallis's fate. The allied troops moved from Williamsburg toward Yorktown on September 28, and within two days the British were completely surrounded. On October 6, General Washington himself turned the first shovelful of earth as his troops began digging siege trenches about 600 yards from the British lines. As the French and Americans edged closer to their opponents, over 100 mortars and cannons daily thundered at the enemy, raining down an incessant bombardment on the outmatched British. On the evening of the fourteenth, American and French troops successfully stormed and captured two outlying British redoubts that had blocked the completion of the allied siege trenches. Once the trenches and batteries were pushed closer to the British, the allied cannoneers kept up the bombardment.

Despairing, Cornwallis decided to cross the York River to Gloucester and drive away the few opposing troops there, then march north toward New York. This desperate plan, although successfully begun, was smashed when a severe storm struck the area on the night of October 16. The next day, when the allied batteries opened an unusually severe assault, Cornwallis hoisted a white flag and requested terms of surrender. The details were quickly worked out, and on the afternoon of October 19, Cornwallis's army marched out to an open field in front of its earthworks and stacked its arms, surrendering 28 unit flags and all of its cannons, with the officers being allowed to retain their swords. More than 7,000 British soldiers surrendered, but Cornwallis was not there. The general sent Washington an apologetic note, claiming that he was sick and could not take part in the surrender ceremony; General Charles O'Hara surrendered the army.

Although the surrender at Yorktown did not end the Revolution, it ended any hope of British success. The war dragged on until 1783, but the major fighting was over. On March 4, 1782, Parliament issued a decree stating that anyone who advocated further offensive prosecution of the war in North America would be considered an enemy of the Crown.

Yorktown itself was a small village surrounded by British earthworks, as depicted by the map below. Allied artillery, aided by French ships, made conditions miserable for the besieged British.

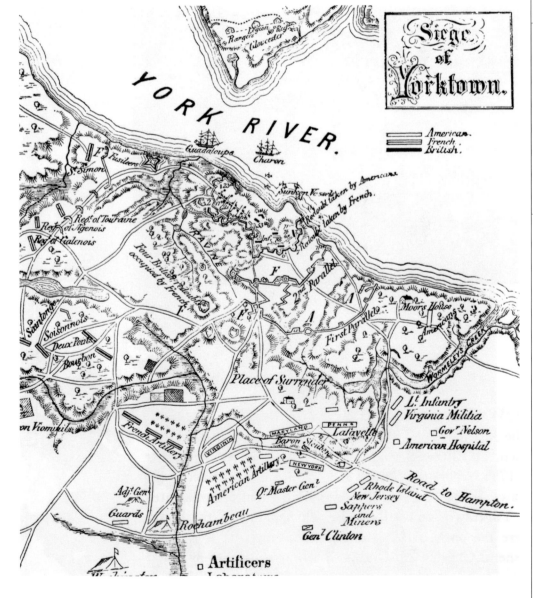

The frigate **USS** *United States*, left, defeats the **HMS** *Macedonian* in a high-sea battle depicted in **William S.** Davis's dramatic scene.

THE WAR OF 1812

1812–1814

American independence, even after a successful revolution, was not secured until almost 30 years afterward. The French Revolution began in 1789 and shortly thereafter Europe became engulfed in wars that lasted until 1815, when Napoleon was finally defeated and sent into exile.

America was caught in the middle of these European wars. Merchant ships were liable to be seized by both French and British ships as each side attempted to interdict the commerce of the other. Furthermore, the English began stopping American ships and impressing sailors, especially those suspected of being deserters from the Royal Navy, to fill their own ships' crews.

1812 United States Army uniforms

The U.S. Brig *Niagara*

The ship that brought Commodore Perry victory was deliberately sunk in 1820 in Misery Bay, across Presque Isle harbor from Erie. The lakes had been demilitarized and there was no need for the ship. In March 1913, the hulk was raised in preparation for the centennial celebration of the battle. Only about 10 percent of the wood was salvageable, and there were no plans of the original vessel found. Still, workers reconstructed a replica of the original *Niagara*. Forgotten afterward, the replica deteriorated so badly that she was again reconstructed in 1943, with help from the Works Progress Administration. But this version of the ship was not finished until 1963, the 150th anniversary of the battle.

Again there was neglect and decay until 1987, when the Pennsylvania Historical and Museum Commission attempted a reconstruction. The replica was demolished; over 100 original timbers were saved and treated. The current version of *Niagara* was completed in 1990, with the addition of a motor for propulsion and other nonhistorical materials to hinder decay.

U.S. Brig **Niagara**

Presidents Thomas Jefferson and James Madison each attempted, without much success, to rectify this deteriorating situation. Embargoes of foreign goods, occasional exchanges of gunfire on the high seas, and repeated American complaints failed to bring either side to respect American

Currier & Ives lithograph of the death of Tecumseh at the Battle of the Thames

neutrality. "The devil himself could not tell which government, England or France, is more wicked," complained Madison.

But many Americans mistrusted England more than France. After all, they had fought the British to obtain their independence, yet the British still haunted the new nation. By treaty, the British were supposed to vacate their forts in the Northwest Territory, but they still had not withdrawn. Their navy acted with contempt toward American ships. Their politicians repeatedly insulted the United States. Their agents fomented Native American hatred toward Americans. Under such threats, a considerable body of "war hawks" in Congress clamored for war. Let America invade Canada and teach the British a lesson!

President Madison tried to avoid war. Military action was not popular throughout the country. Merchants in New England were bitter critics of the government's embargo policies and wanted open trade. But westerners and southerners thought otherwise. Finally, on June 1, 1812, Madison presented a war message to Congress,

leaving it up to that body to declare war; Madison himself refused to commit the country to an armed struggle. By June 17, Congress had voted for war. Unbeknownst to America, on June 23, the English government revoked most of those orders considered inflammatory to Americans, but slow communications meant that war had begun in spite of efforts to avoid it.

The War of 1812 pitted America against England, which, preoccupied with Napoleon, could not commit its vast resources across the Atlantic. Fighting took place in the Northwest Territory, where General William Henry Harrison defeated a British invasion of Ohio. Then, after Commodore Oliver Hazard Perry's decisive naval victory on Lake Erie in September 1813, Harrison invaded Canada, defeating a British army at the Battle of the Thames, where Native American chief Tecumseh was slain.

On the Niagara front, a series of sharp, vicious battles occurred throughout 1812–14. The end result was a stalemate, as the sides were evenly matched and protected by strong fortifications that made a decisive victory impossible. The opposing naval commanders on Lake Ontario built bigger and bigger warships to win a battle that never occurred.

On the high seas, American frigates such as the *Constitution*, *United States*, and *Constellation* won victories over British warships, which gave Americans something to cheer about. But, as the war dragged on, more and more British ships were committed to America, blockading the outnumbered Americans in their harbors.

Once Napoleon was overthrown, the British were able to send more troops to America. One such expedition entered Chesapeake Bay in the summer of 1814. This force landed near Washington, defeated the defending troops, then captured the city and burned government buildings, including the Executive Mansion. Once repaired and repainted, it was soon nicknamed the "White House." The ensuing British attack on Baltimore was repelled, and the enemy withdrew from the Chesapeake.

In the South, Andrew Jackson, general of the Tennessee militia, decisively defeated the Creek Indians at Horseshoe Bend in March 1814. Jackson was then placed in command of the entire Southern Department, with orders to defend the vital port of New Orleans. A British army of more than 14,000 veterans landed in December and marched toward the city, which was defended by Jackson with some 4,500 American Regulars, militia, Native Americans, free blacks, and Jean Lafitte's pirates. General Sir Edward Packenham attacked on January 2, 1815; Americans, fighting from behind cotton bales, repelled the British, inflicting a loss of 2,000 against only 45 for themselves. But, on December 24, 1814, American and British negotiators had already signed a peace treaty in Ghent, Belgium. Jackson's victory was actually fought after the war had officially ended, but the decisive nature of this battle was a much-needed tonic for flagging American spirits.

Considered by some the "Second American Revolution," the War of 1812 ensured independence for the United States and brought respect to the young nation.

JEAN LAFITTE

Jean Lafitte was a pirate who played a key role in Andrew Jackson's victory at New Orleans. No one knew where he had come from—it was probably the Caribbean—but by 1809 Lafitte had come to Louisiana.

By 1810, Lafitte controlled a band of pirates based at Barataria Bay, on the Gulf Coast south of New Orleans. Even though the U.S. Navy raided his base and the governor of Louisiana put a price on his head, Lafitte resisted British offers of aid and passed their plans on to Jackson. In return for full pardons, Lafitte offered his pirates as allies against the British. Jackson agreed, and Lafitte's men manned American artillery and supplied weapons and ammunition that tipped the scales in Jackson's favor during the January 8, 1815, battle.

Though pardoned by Jackson, Lafitte quickly returned to piracy, moving his base to Galveston Island, Texas. When the U.S. Navy again proved a threat, Lafitte sailed away in 1821. He and his band were never heard from again.

General Jackson's victory at New Orleans

Jean Lafitte

PERRY'S VICTORY

INTERNATIONAL PEACE MEMORIAL

Commodore Oliver Hazard Perry had been given the Herculean task of building an American fleet to control Lake Erie. He gathered men and supplies at Erie, Pennsylvania, and began work in early 1813, his base under constant scrutiny by British captain Robert H. Barclay's ships. Perry had his fleet ready by early August, then sailed west in search of the enemy. Perry commanded two brigs—the *Lawrence* (his flagship) and the *Niagara*—four schooners, and three smaller ships, mounting a total of 54 guns, primarily short-range carronades. Barclay had the *Queen Charlotte* and *Detroit*, also two brigs, one schooner, and one sloop, mounting 63 guns in all.

The opposing fleets sighted each other early on September 10. The British ships concentrated their fire on the *Lawrence*, wrecking the vessel and rendering her useless. Mysteriously, Perry's second-in-command, Captain Jesse D. Elliott, kept the *Niagara* out of the first phase of the battle. Perry heroically took a small rowboat across to the *Niagara* and assumed command. As the *Niagara* bore down on the British, *Queen Charlotte* and the *Detroit* collided as they tried to maneuver into firing positions. While the British crews tried to disentangle their vessels, Perry steered and raked the enemy with close-range broadsides for 15 crucial minutes. As the other American ships engaged their counterparts, a wounded Barclay struck his colors. Perry captured all six British ships, thus gaining naval superiority on the lake. This enabled General William Henry Harrison to launch an offensive that carried his army into Canada and a victory at the Thames River on October 5.

With the end of the war, America and Canada, by the terms of the Rush-Bagot Treaty of 1817, demilitarized the Great Lakes. To commemorate Perry's victory and the treaty, nine states and the federal government contributed money for the International Peace Memorial, built between 1912 and 1915. Composed of pink granite from Massachusetts, this imposing Doric column stands 352 feet high, surmounted by an 11-ton bronze urn. The monument was built on South Bass Island, some three miles from the mainland, and can be reached by ferry from April through October.

Perry's Victory and International Peace Memorial

Battle of Lake Erie depicted by artist Percy Moran. With his flagship *Lawrence* a wreck, Commodore Oliver H. Perry lowered one of the ship's lifeboats and was rowed over to the U.S. Brig *Niagara*—the key move that led to the American victory.

Long after its moment of glory in 1814, Fort McHenry continued to be the main point of defense for Baltimore. This scene shows a Union infantry regiment drawn up in parade formation sometime during the Civil War, when the fort was used mainly as a holding place for political prisoners.

FORT McHENRY
THE ROCKETS' RED GLARE

French emperor Napoleon abdicated in April 1814. Great Britain was now able to reinforce the troops that had been fighting the Americans since 1812. British plans called for a three-pronged advance in key areas—Lake Champlain, New Orleans, and Chesapeake Bay. Vice Admiral Sir Alexander Cochrane's formidable fleet of 50 warships carried an army contingent of 4,600, led by Major General Robert Ross.

This British force sailed across the Atlantic and entered Chesapeake Bay in August 1814. The young nation's capital, Washington, was its first target. Ross's troops landed east of Washington and engaged the defending force in Maryland on August 24. The Battle of Bladensburg was a resounding defeat for the Americans, who, even though outnumbering the enemy, were mostly untried militia that fled when pressed. Ross's troops entered the capital even as President James Madison and his family fled. The Executive Mansion and other government buildings were burned in retaliation for destruction of Canadian government buildings in York (modern Toronto) by American troops a year earlier.

Baltimore was the next British objective. More than 15,000 troops under the command of Revolutionary War veteran Major General Samuel Smith had built earthworks around the city to protect it against a land attack. Most of Smith's troops were militia from surrounding states, but under his command were a few units from the Regular Army and Commodore John Rodgers's stranded sailors.

The key to the city's defenses was Fort McHenry, situated to protect Northwest Branch, the main channel into Baltimore Harbor. This brick fort, built between 1798 and 1805, mounted 60 cannons, including 18-, 24-, and 36-pounders. Major George Armistead commanded the Fort McHenry garrison, which included a disorganized company of Regular Army artillerists and four local militia companies. Two companies of Sea Fencibles and sailors from Commodore Joshua Barney's flotilla also contributed to the fort's defense. Detachments of three Regular Army regiments protected the fort from an infantry attack. Armistead's troops totaled about

Fort McHenry

THE FATE OF THE STAR-SPANGLED BANNER

Major Armistead kept Fort McHenry's flag in his family over the years, but occasionally allowed it to be used in ceremonies. The flag was eventually loaned to the United States in 1907; in 1912, the family made it a gift to the people of America. The banner was soon displayed in the Smithsonian Institution. It was sewn onto linen backing for reinforcement, but over the years light, dirt, and other factors contributed to its slow yet steady deterioration. Souvenir hunters had clipped off portions of the banner, so that it now is about 8 feet shorter than when originally constructed. In 1996, concern over its continued survival brought together a panel of 50 national flag experts—historians and conservators—who worked out a detailed plan for its conservation and future display.

The Star-Spangled Banner prior to reconstruction

> ## "... from 15 to 1800 shells were thrown by the enemy. A few fell short. A large proportion burst over us, throwing their fragments among us ... our loss amounts only to four men killed, and 24 wounded."
>
> —*Major George Armistead, commanding Fort McHenry*

1,000 officers and troops. A few gunboats lent support, and the wreckage of vessels that had been sunk off the entrance to Northwest Branch effectively blocked an easy passage.

Vice Admiral Cochrane realized that Fort McHenry had to be neutralized in order to capture Baltimore. Meanwhile Major General Ross landed his troops on September 12 at North Point, then marched them north toward the American earthworks. Ross was mortally wounded later that afternoon as his men skirmished with Americans sent out to delay his advance. Colonel Arthur Brooke took command and pushed the Americans back into their earthworks. He then halted to await word of the fleet's success.

Cochrane brought his ships forward and opened fire on Fort McHenry shortly after dawn on September 13. The British used a half-dozen ships altered to fire heavy siege mortars. Projectiles from these weapons, with a range of 2 miles, arced high overhead and dropped on the defenders from above. Cochrane also used the newly designed Congreve rocket, an inaccurate weapon whose major ingredient was terror, so instigated by its screeching noise and speed. The bombardment vessels drew up in line about 2 miles from the fort, just out of effective range of the shorter-range American smooth-bore cannons.

The British bombardment continued all day and on into the night. Rain and darkness hampered assessment of their own bombardment. Cochrane sent out a landing party up Ferry Branch in order to distract the Americans long enough for Brooke to launch a land attack. However, the dark night and unfamiliar terrain disoriented the British, who were discovered and driven back.

Realizing that his shelling was not proving effective, Cochrane called a halt to the firing around seven o'clock on the morning of September 14. That morning, as usual, the fort fired its morning gun, hauled down the wet ensign that flew during the battle, then hoisted an over-large 32 x 40-foot American flag to show the British that Americans were still full of fight.

This is the flag that Francis Scott Key immortalized. Key, a Washington lawyer, accompanied by Colonel John S. Skinner, American Commissioner General of Prisoners, had sailed out to the British fleet under a white flag. The two Americans wished to negotiate the release of Dr. William Beanes, a civilian who had been captured at Bladensburg, released, then recaptured near Baltimore and accused of violating his good conduct pledge. Skinner and Key were successful in their quest, but were restrained from leaving until after the British bombardment; Cochrane refused to allow the Americans to inform their compatriots of British plans.

Thus, during the bombardment, the American truce ship remained well to the rear, among the British fleet. Key spent a restless night as the British bombardment lit up the sky with bursting mortar shells and Congreve rockets streaking across

Francis Scott Key watching the bombardment of Fort McHenry

the night sky, followed by the occasional American reply. He later recalled his view at dawn, when the American garrison hoisted its flag: "Through the clouds of the war the stars of that banner still shone in my view, and I saw the discomfited host of its assailants driven back in ignominy to their ships. Then, in the hour of deliverance, and joyful triumph, my heart spoke; and 'Does not such a country and such defenders of their country deserve a song?' was its question."

Key immediately jotted down some notes and within two days had completed a poem entitled "Defence of Fort McHenry." The *Baltimore Patriot* published the poem, which quickly was adopted to the tune "To Anacreon in Heaven." The song eventually was retitled "The Star-Spangled Banner" and in 1931 became America's official national anthem.

Fort McHenry's flag went on to become one of America's most beloved and recognized treasures. Major Armistead had contracted with Baltimore flag maker Mary Pickersgill to produce a flag large enough that the British would have "no difficulty seeing it from a distance." Her flag, made of wool bunting with 15 stars and 15 stripes, measured an incredible 30 x 42 feet. Mrs. Pickersgill and her 13-year-old daughter Caroline cut fabric and sewed the pieces together on the floor of a Baltimore malthouse because the flag was too big for her small abode. The bill for time, labor, and materials came to $405.90.

Fort McHenry's moment of fame was its only time under hostile fire. When Civil War broke out in 1861, the fort was quickly garrisoned by Union troops, who installed water batteries and stood guard to defend Baltimore against a Confederate attack. Throughout the conflict, it was used to house political prisoners, Southern sympathizers, and a few Confederate prisoners of war. The fort remained an active-duty installation for decades after the 1860s. In 1925, Fort McHenry became a national park; in 1939, it was redesignated a national monument and historic shrine, the only national park so honored.

JOHN BURNS

In August 1814, as British forces sailed into Chesapeake Bay, the 2nd Pennsylvania militia was among a force of almost 10,000 men gathered together at Marcus Hook, 20 miles south of Philadelphia on the Delaware River. The British were rebuffed at Baltimore, and the 2nd Pennsylvania was disbanded in December. Among the unit's men was John L. Burns, a 20-year-old son of Scottish immigrants. After the war, Burns migrated west to Adams County. On July 1, 1863, as Union troops took positions west of Gettysburg, Burns, then almost 70 years old, appeared at the front and volunteered his assistance. Securing a rifle and ammunition, he took a minor part in the fighting until wounded late that afternoon. When President Lincoln came to Gettysburg in November to dedicate its cemetery, he went to church with Burns and propelled the aged veteran to national fame. In 1903, a monument honoring Burns was dedicated on the Gettysburg battlefield.

John Burns

VISITOR INFORMATION

Name Boston

Classification National Historical Park

Established October 21, 1797. Restored in 1927, moored at Charlestown Navy Yard since 1934. Transferred to Boston National Historical Park in 1974

Contact Charlestown Navy Yard, Boston, MA 02129

Phone 617-242-5642

Website www.nps.gov/bost/Navy_Yard.htm

Acreage N/A

Points of Focus Chain Forge, Dry Dock 1, Ropewalk

Tours/Paths Self-guided walking tours, Ranger-guided walking tours

Hours Open daily from 10:00 A.M. to 4:00 P.M. April 1 to October 31; closed on Mondays for maintenance; November 1 to March 31; closed Monday – Wednesday for maintenance and training

Park Fee Free

Programs "Serving the Fleet" exhibit program

Facilities USS *Constitution* Museum, information center

USS CONSTITUTION

OLD IRONSIDES

Launched in 1797, the USS *Constitution* was one of six wooden frigates authorized by George Washington to protect the young nation's merchant fleet from attacks by Mediterranean pirates. Built of wood obtained from several eastern states and fitted with copper fastenings crafted by Paul Revere, the *Constitution* was constructed in Boston at a cost of $302,700. The new vessel served in the 1798–1801 quasi-war with France and saw action against the Barbary pirates in 1803–1805.

With the outbreak of war with England in 1812, the *Constitution* provided America with two important victories in a year of defeats on land. The first took place on August 19, when Captain Isaac Hull engaged the British frigate *Guerriere* in the northern Atlantic. After the two vessels maneuvered into firing range, the ships fired their guns. In half an hour, *Guerriere* lost all her masts and her captain surrendered. As a result of this battle, the *Constitution* earned the nickname "Old Ironsides." British cannonballs had reputedly bounced off her sides during the battle, causing a crewman to exclaim, "Her sides are made of iron!"

On December 29, while cruising off the coast of Brazil in search of British merchant ships, the *Constitution* encountered the British frigate *Java*. Now under the command of Captain William Bainbridge, the *Constitution* suffered some damage, but Bainbridge skilfully maneuvered his ship for more than three hours. By then, *Java's* Captain Henry Lambert had been mortally wounded and all her masts shot down, with 130 casualties on her decks. *Java* surrendered to Bainbridge, whose crew counted 34 sailors dead and wounded.

During the rest of the war the *Constitution* captured some British merchantmen but, like the rest of the small American navy, was often blockaded in port by the larger British navy. In February 1815, Captain Charles Stewart outmaneuvered two British warships and forced their surrender, one last American victory before the conflict was over. Congress honored Stewart, Hull, and Bainbridge with gold medals. The *Constitution* was the only ship thus honored during the war.

Action between the Constitution and the Guerriere

Landlubbers seeing this bow view of the USS *Constitution* are amazed at the number of ropes that appear to go in every direction. But each of these lines has a purpose, and crew members were taught what each was used for.

U.S. Army troops accompany members of the five "civilized" tribes on their journey from ancestral lands in the South to new homes across the Mississippi River in present-day Oklahoma. This "Trail of Tears" left thousands dead in the forced migration.

THE EXPANSION

1804—1892

From the first explorations of the North American continent to the end of the nineteenth century, settlers arriving in the New World had to contend with the Native American population in a variety of ways. Some English colonies (Pennsylvania and Maryland, for example) had relatively peaceful relations at first. Others—owing to disputes over land rights, lack of respect for native culture, and other reasons—had stormy relations with natives who encountered an increasing number of foreigners invading their shores.

Indeed, the story of white–Native American relations is one of frequent betrayal, atrocities, sorrow, and tragedy. Early attempts to befriend and

surveying compass

CAMELS

In 1855, acting on Secretary of War Jefferson Davis's report, Congress appropriated money to buy camels in the Middle East, transport them to America, and test their utility in the army by using them in the deserts of the American Southwest. In all, some 74 camels were brought to America, along with several drivers. The U.S. Camel Corps began operation in 1857, working from western Texas and the territories of New Mexico and Arizona to California. But the advent of civil war in 1861 doomed the corps. The Confederacy seized some of the camels, while those in American possession were auctioned off. Reports of wild camels surfaced as late as 1941. Every January, the Arizona town of Quartzsite celebrates camels with a series of special events.

Haiji Ali's Tomb in Quartzsite, Arizona, marks the grave of the Assyrian camel jockey known as "Hi Jolly," who stayed in America and lived until 1902.

assist confused settlers were repaid by rapine, slaughter, seizure of homelands, and forced migration. When Native Americans struck back, they were generally the losers, such as in King Philip's War (1675–76), the first major native counterattack against colonial America. During the wars between England and France for hegemony in North America, Native Americans fought with both sides, often to their detriment no matter who won these conflicts. Parliament's attempt to prevent westward expansion of England's 13 American colonies—and thus avoid sustained hostilities between natives and settlers—was one of many grievances against England. During the Revolution Native Americans again took part on both sides and wound up losing much of their land and independence as a result of America's victory.

One need for a standing army in the decades after independence was that of protecting Americans from native attacks. Although New England tribes had been decimated in the years since the 1670s, powerful tribes in the Midwest and South at times stymied westward expansion. A series of conflicts prior to the War of 1812 broke the back of opposition in the Midwest, but the mighty Creek nation in the Southeast obstructed new settlement. However, in 1814, Andrew Jackson campaigned actively against the Creeks and in March decisively defeated them at Horseshoe Bend, Alabama. The peace treaty Creeks signed gave the United States much of its homeland. Jackson, who later became president,

Native Americans attacking a wagon train

used forced migration to remove five civilized tribes from the South to reservations in present-day Oklahoma. The "Trail of Tears" that resulted meant starvation and death for thousands of Native Americans.

As the expanding nation reached the edge of the Great Plains, settlers encountered Native American tribes that had adopted the use of horses bred from animals left behind by early Spanish explorers. Their mobility and tenacious defense of tribal lands resulted in a series of wars and years of desultory skirmishing between the tribes, the United States Army, and settlers. The army built a series of forts along the frontier as it tried to contain the Native Americans and also prevent unruly settlers from breaking the terms of previous peace treaties.

American success in the Mexican War (1845–47) brought the boundary of the country almost to its present state, adding Texas, New Mexico, Arizona, and California to the United States. The conflict with Mexico originated with war hawks in Congress eager to expand America's boundaries, and perhaps slavery as well. A boundary dispute involving the southern border of Texas brought the two countries into open warfare in 1845. The first two battles of the war—Palo Alto and Resaca de la Palma—took place in Texas when a Mexican army division crossed the Rio Grande and engaged General Zachary Taylor's troops in combat. General Winfield Scott then led a successful campaign that captured Mexico City and brought hostilities to an end.

The discovery of gold in California in 1847 and the resulting migration of thousands of Americans across the plains intensified the warfare. During the Civil War, Native American soldiers enlisted on both sides and fought in a number of battles west of the Mississippi. After the war, however, in large part due to the Homestead Act, to westward railroad expansion, and to other postwar legislation, a new wave of settlers erupted onto the plains, sparking a number of deadly encounters with native groups.

Certain post–Civil War engagements typified the ongoing war between Native Americans and the United States. Between 1865 and 1891 the U.S. Army conducted 13 campaigns against the natives, engaging them in 1,067 separate actions. One authority has tallied army casualties as 948 killed and 1,058 wounded. Meanwhile, Native American casualties in these battles have been estimated at 4,371 killed, 1,279 wounded, and 10,318 captured. The Bureau of Indian Affairs was responsible for maintaining law and order and providing for Native Americans who peacefully remained on reservations established by peace treaties. Often gold and other precious metals were found on native land and greedy settlers broke the treaties by illegally trespassing on native real estate; when the occupants fought back, the army intervened, and politicians in Washington sided with the lawbreakers. The losers proved to be innocent victims—Native Americans—who saw their land continue to shrink.

Some army officers (such as John Pope) sympathized with the natives, while others, such as Philip Sheridan and William T. Sherman, were openly hostile to them. Subordinates who tried to prevent bloodshed were often caught in the middle, torn between duty and sympathy.

Later in the nineteenth century fighting swirled from Texas to the Canadian border and as far west as the Pacific Coast. Major tribes involved included the Cheyenne, Arapohoes, Kiowa, Commanches, Modocs, Nez Perce, Sioux (Lakota), Apaches, Utes, and others. Their leaders included the most famous names in Native American history—Red Cloud, Black Kettle, Captain Jack, Chief Joseph, Sitting Bull, Cochise, Geronimo, and Victorio. Arrayed against them were the army's most colorful leaders—George Armstrong Custer, Alfred Terry, George Crook, Ranald Mackenzie, Nelson Miles, and John Gibbon.

At times, neither side took prisoners and butchered each other ferociously. More often than not, army officers destroyed buffalo and pony herds as well as murdering old men, women, and children during attacks on native encampments. Contemporary literature often portrayed the Native American warriors as bloodthirsty savages, eager to take white women captive while scalping their husbands. Much purple prose was spilled in recounting the famous tale of Custer and his 7th United States Cavalry being decimated by its defeat at Little Bighorn on June 25, 1876.

By the time the 7th Cavalry massacred Sioux villagers at Wounded Knee, South Dakota, on December 29, 1890, the American frontier was largely a thing of the past. Settlers had swarmed across western America, confining Native Americans who survived to a series of reservations, often minuscule pieces of their ancestral homelands. Open warfare was over, but the pain and memory of repeated defeats, loss of ancestral lands, and cultural degradation remain sore topics among Native American tribes.

Major Samuel Ringgold at the Battle of Palo Alto

Fort Marion has a rich history. Built in 1672 as an outpost of the Spanish Empire, who called it **Castillo de San Marcos**, it was the first permanent European settlement in the continental United States. Control of the fort changed several times from Spanish to British and back to Spanish until 1821, when the land was purchased by the United States and the fort was officially named Fort Marion.

FORTS

SENTINELS OF THE FRONTIER

The purpose for which forts were built dictated their construction and shape. Along the East Coast, where defense was of paramount concern, there were three waves of construction. The so-called first system consisted mainly of earthwork berms hurriedly built during and after the Revolutionary War. These quickly fell into disrepair. After the War of 1812, a second system consisted of forts with masonry walls facing the sea and some protection from the land side. The third system, begun in 1817, was a permanent coastal defense system of brick and masonry forts with multi-tiered batteries of heavy guns. To offer maximum fields of fire, many forts were star-shaped where terrain allowed. All were built to withstand naval attacks launched by European powers.

In the American West, the needs were more immediate and their purpose was different. Forts in the West were mostly rectangular log stockades. They offered protection from an enemy that possessed no artillery and they served as bases for offensive forays by soldiers assigned the duty of policing a large territory.

The first European settlers who arrived in North America erected forts to protect themselves from Native Americans and other inimical groups of settlers. Most of these early protections were no more than log palisades designed to temporarily house the population of a village in case of attack. In colonial times, many frontier forts were simply reinforced log structures loopholed to allow defenders to fire on attackers. When professional military engineers were involved, though, forts assumed the air of their European counterparts. Examples include Fort Ticonderoga in New York and the Spanish fort at Saint Augustine, Florida.

The new American nation constructed forts to protect itself from both Native Americans and foreign aggression. Over the years, coastal fortifications were erected to protect vulnerable harbors from enemy fleets and troops—Fort Sumter in Charleston Harbor and Fort McHenry in Baltimore Harbor are two examples.

When settlers reached the Great Plains the army constructed forts to protect civilians as well as to provide bases of supply for operations against Native American tribes. Most of these frontier forts were not the massive timbered structures with blockhouses that are familiar to moviegoers. Instead, many were simply structures erected around a central parade ground, often without protecting walls. Many were occupied only until their location and usefulness were outgrown by the progress of the frontier.

Some of these forts—such as Fort Leavenworth, Kansas—are still active-duty posts. A number are preserved so that visitors can see how the army policed the frontier. Fort Smith, Arkansas, was active from 1817 until 1871 and served as a central supply post for other forts throughout the southwestern United States. Fort Scott, Kansas, was built in 1842 and abandoned in 1855. The post was again manned in 1861 and finally closed in 1873. Fort Union, New Mexico, went through two major renovations and locations before it was closed in 1891. Fort Bowie, Arizona, was built during the Civil War to control the strategic Apache Pass. This fort was the central base for operations against the Apache Nation before its closure in 1894.

Clash with Sioux Indians outside Fort Union

VISITOR INFORMATION

Name Palo Alto Battlefield

Classification National Historic Site

Established November 10, 1978. Boundary change: June 23, 1992

Contact 1623 Central Blvd., #213, Brownsville, TX 78520

Phone 956-541-2785

Website www.nps.gov/paal

Acreage 3,357.42 (Federal: 1,039.62; Nonfederal: 2,317.80)

Points of Focus Site is well preserved but has limited access at present. Visitors should stop at the temporary visitor center in Brownsville for more information.

Tours/Paths Walking trail

Hours Open weekdays from 8:30 A.M. to 4:00 P.M. Closed on weekends and all federal holidays

Park Fee Free

Programs 15-minute orientation film, Junior Ranger program

Facilities Visitor center, bookstore

PALO ALTO
THE BATTLE FOR TEXAS

The republic of Texas revolted from Mexico and secured its independence in 1836. Although Americans generally supported Texas's bid for freedom, the 1830s political climate discouraged its admission as a state. However, by the mid-1840s views had begun to change, and President James K. Polk recommended annexation in March 1845. Mexico accordingly withdrew its ambassador and protested American involvement in determining the territory's status. When Texas was admitted as a state in December 1845, its boundary was in question. Texas claimed the Rio Grande; Mexico said the boundary was the Neuces River.

In March 1846, General Zachary Taylor arrived on the Rio Grande with some 2,000 American Regulars. His engineers constructed Fort Texas (later renamed Fort Brown) on the site of present-day Brownsville as a base camp. Taylor's supplies came by sea from New Orleans, so the general kept troops to guard this vulnerable stretch of territory. The Mexicans countered by dispatch-ing General Mariano Arista and 6,000 troops to watch the Americans.

On April 25, Mexicans crossed the Rio Grande and ambushed an American reconnaissance party. President Polk used this incident to request a declaration of war, issued by Congress on May 13.

The first battle of the war actually took place on May 8, before official declaration. General Taylor had moved most of his troops to the coast to secure new supplies before escorting them back to Fort Texas. In the meantime Mexicans besieged the fort, but Major Jacob Brown's garrison repelled the attackers. As Taylor's troops drew near, Arista arrayed his larger army across a broad prairie and awaited the Americans. Taylor attacked on May 8 at Palo Alto. His artillery pounded the Mexican lines as his infantry repelled several Mexican frontal assaults. Finally, Taylor ordered an advance and the Mexicans retreated. They had suffered a loss of more than 225 as compared to 51 American casualties.

Arista chose to fight again the next day at Resaca de la Palma. Again the Americans prevailed. Arista's men fled the field and the victors gathered up all sorts of bounty from the Mexican baggage train. Arista's army lost more than 500 men, while there were 154 American casualties. Fort Texas was saved and Texas cleared of the enemy.

General Taylor at the Battle of Palo Alto

Major Ringgold's death at Palo Alto early in the war, depicted by this contemporary lithograph, became a well-known event. Ringgold was the first officer killed in the Mexican War.

Black Kettle's people were completely surprised and offered little resistance at first. Rampaging soldiers fired at any Native American they saw, be it man, woman, or child.

WASHITA

BATTLE OR MASSACRE?

VISITOR INFORMATION

Name Washita Battlefield

Classification National Historic Site

Established November 12, 1996

Contact P.O. Box 890, Cheyenne, OK 73628

Phone 580-497-2742

Website www.nps.gov/waba

Acreage 315.20 (Federal: 312.20; Nonfederal: 3.0)

Points of Focus Monument, historical plaque, trailhead

Tours/Paths 1.5-mile self-guided walking tour, Ranger-led walks

Hours Park headquarters open on weekdays from 8:00 A.M. to 5:00 P.M. Closed all federal holidays

Park Fee Free

Programs Ranger-led programs (summer season only), Junior Ranger program

Facilities Black Kettle Museum, park headquarters, picnic area

Just before dawn on November 27, 1868, Lieutenant Colonel George A. Custer and his 7th United States Cavalry swooped down on a Cheyenne village situated along the Washita River. He was acting under the orders of his superior, General Philip A. Sheridan, who was determined to squash the Cheyenne in spite of peace efforts by their chief, Black Kettle. A white woman and her child had been kidnapped, and although it was uncertain which tribe had done this, Sheridan wanted to make an example of the Cheyenne.

The cavalry charge through the village completely surprised the Cheyenne warriors. After scattering the occupants, Custer's men regrouped and spent several hours chasing down and shooting fugitives. Custer claimed to have slain 103 warriors, but critics reduced this number to 11; the remaining dead were old men, women, and children, all indiscriminately shot by the soldiers. Black Kettle and his wife were killed as they fled.

After securing all the loot desired by his troops, Custer ordered the village burned before they departed. The entire Native American herd of some 800 mules and ponies, excepting those animals seized to mount the 53 captives taken, was then destroyed. Custer was unable to locate Major Joel Elliott and 18 troopers who had disappeared. Two weeks later, when the cavalry again visited the site, they found Elliott and his men, all dead. The major had fled the Cheyenne, only to encounter swarms of warriors moving north to the battle site, attracted by the firing. Custer had failed to reconnoiter and was unaware of other tribes wintering in the area.

Contemporaries hailed Custer's victory. He had shown the hostiles what would happen should they continue to raid frontier settlements. The bodies of the kidnapped woman and her child were found during a closer examination of bodies at the site, but controversy surrounds this discovery as well. An army general who was negotiating for her release castigated Custer for fouling up his efforts. Black Kettle's tribe had evidently had nothing to do with her abduction. With the assage of time, Custer's actions seem less and less like warfare and more like a massacre.

Prisoners from Black Kettle's camp captured by Lieutenant Colonel Custer

LITTLE BIGHORN

CUSTER'S LAST STAND

Without a doubt, the Battle of Little Bighorn on June 25, 1876, is one of the most storied yet controversial engagements in American history. On that fateful day, Lieutenant Colonel George A. Custer divided his companies of the 7th United States Cavalry in the face of a numerically superior foe. Custer and his detachment were wiped out; the cavalry suffered a loss of 263 killed and 52 wounded.

The friction between Native Americans of the Lakota (Sioux) and Cheyenne tribes and white settlers stemmed partly from the discovery of gold in the Black Hills of South Dakota, an integral part of the reservation granted to the Lakota by an 1868 treaty. The army tried to keep the settlers out; the government tried to buy the ancestral land from the Native Americans. American railroads were also being built on Lakota land without their permission. While Custer tried to protect the railroads' interests, the Sioux were defending their land from American invasion. Angered, hundreds of warriors left the reservation and began raiding frontier settlements.

A soldier's headstone at the battlefield

In December 1875, the commissioner of Indian Affairs ordered all hostiles to return to the reservation before January 31, 1876, or thereafter be compelled by military force.

Lack of compliance by Native Americans led to the military campaign of 1876. Three separate expeditions converged on tribes concentrated in southeastern Montana under the leadership of Sitting Bull, Crazy Horse, Gall, and other chiefs.

General George Crook led one column of troops north from Fort Fetterman in Wyoming. Colonel John Gibbon commanded an infantry column from Fort Ellis northeast along the Yellowstone River, while General Alfred H. Terry brought a third column west from Fort Abraham Lincoln.

Crook's men encountered superior numbers of Native Americans and fought a losing battle on the Rosebud River on June 17; Crook withdrew under pressure. Terry and Gibbon joined forces at the confluence of the Yellowstone and Rosebud, then decided to part ways. Gibbon, accompanied by Terry, backtracked to the Bighorn River, then headed south toward Crook's reported location. Custer's 7th Cavalry

In 1876, Custer's men, as this reenactment portrays, were armed with revolvers and carbines; for the campaign, their cavalry swords were packed away. Recent archaeological investigations on the battlefield after brush fires burned off prairie sod and undergrowth revealed a host of spent cartridges, showing that the Native Americans often had better arms.

GEORGE A. CUSTER

The victim of "Custer's Last Stand" has been a popular figure in American history writing. Custer graduated last in the West Point class of June 1861. After months as an unremarkable staff officer in the Army of the Potomac, he garnered a job as a cavalry staff officer. On June 28, 1863, Custer was jumped from captain to brigadier general in charge of a brigade of Michigan troops, which he led brilliantly in the Gettysburg Campaign. By war's end, Custer was a major general in command of a division.

After the Civil War, Custer reverted to the rank of lieutenant colonel in field command of the new 7th U.S. Cavalry. He was shelved for a year without rank and pay for shooting deserters without trial and abandoning his command. Still, higher officers brought the aggressive Custer back to duty. His operations against hostile Indian tribes earned him both respect and hatred among his enemies. Custer's defeat in 1876 led to a lively scholarly debate over whether or not he had disobeyed orders, and even debate as to the possibility that he committed suicide that fateful day.

*Lieutenant Colonel
George A. Custer*

*Lieutenant Colonel George Armstrong Custer and five companies of the 7th Cavalry are wiped out by the Sioux and Cheyenne
at the Battle of Little Bighorn, Montana*

headed south along the Rosebud to Little Bighorn, then went north to join Gibbon's column.

Custer's scouts located the Native American camps along Little Bighorn early on June 25. The lieutenant colonel probably underestimated the size of the encampment (as many as 7,000 people, with 1,500 to 2,000 warriors) when he divided his regiment into three battalions. Custer himself took five companies to assail the lower end of the camp. Major Marcus A. Reno's three companies were ordered to cross the river and charge the other end of the camp, while Major Frederick W. Benteen and three companies were sent to scout to the south. A single company was placed in charge of the regiment's pack train.

Reno charged into the edge of the encampment, only to meet scores of warriors riding out to meet him. The major attempted to make a stand, but his outnumbered men were forced back across the river with hundreds of hostiles in hot pursuit. Reno managed to rally his shaken troopers and take up a position on a wooded bluff overlooking the river, where his men dug rifle pits and held off attacking Lakota warriors.

Reno was soon joined by Major Benteen's battalion. Benteen had received a terse message from Custer: "Come on; Big village, be quick, bring packs." Benteen tried to obey Custer's directive but encountered swarms of warriors in his own path. He managed to find Reno, and their combined forces dug in and held off the enemy. The two majors simultaneously gathered their men and headed off toward Custer's position, only to find tribesmen in their way. Heavy firing to the north indicated Custer's command was also engaged, but as the remaining companies approached, the firing stopped and they were assailed by increasing numbers of warriors. Reno and Benteen withdrew to their original position, dug in, and repelled several attempts to storm their hill. The seven companies remained under fire all day, through the night, and into the next day, when the tribesmen withdrew. Terry and Gibbon soon arrived, their approach having been the reason for the Lakota withdrawal.

Once the battlefield was silent, the remaining soldiers headed north and found Custer's body, surrounded by the five companies under his command. There were no survivors, but afterward, when peace had been reinstated, it was possible to speak with Lakota who had taken part in the battle in

Captain Myles Keough's horse, Comanche, one of the equine survivors of the Custer debacle

order to arrive at a reasonable synopsis of events. Custer's troopers had also encountered hordes of warriors as his men tried to attack the camp. Custer had withdrawn to higher ground east of the river, where his companies had been surrounded and annihilated. Their generally naked and mutilated bodies were found on June 26, when Reno and Benteen's men roamed over the field looking for Custer.

The Battle of Little Bighorn was an overwhelming victory for the Lakota, but they won the battle and lost the war. Their casualties were light, perhaps 100 killed, as opposed to the 315 cavalry troopers killed and wounded in Custer's, Reno's and Benteen's commands, but in their haste to get away from the area, the encampment broke up. Some fled north into Canada, others returned to the reservation, and those who kept on the run eventually surrendered to the army troops committed to the war.

Custer and his men were buried on the battlefield where they fell. Eventually, Custer's remains were reinterred and buried at West Point. In 1881, the remains of most of his soldiers were gathered together into a mass grave, and in 1890 government tombstones were erected to show the original location of each burial. A few cavalry horses survived the carnage. The most famous is Comanche, the charger of Captain Myles Keough of Company I. Though wounded, Comanche was recognized as Keough's horse and nursed back to health. He became the mascot of the 7th Cavalry and after his death, his body was stuffed and mounted for permanent display in the regiment's museum.

The battlefield continues to engender controversy to this day. It lies in the midst of the Crow Indian Reservation, and the method of the site's interpretation has led to much controversy with Native Americans. Since 1999, the National Park Service has allowed the erection of three monuments to mark the locations where three Lakota warriors fell during the 1876 battle.

SITTING BULL

The great Lakota chief Sitting Bull was probably born in 1831. By the 1870s, he had risen to be the primary leader of the Lakota (Sioux) and was a major factor in the decision to oppose forced settlement on reservations after the discovery of gold on their ancestral lands. His forces defeated Custer in 1876, but the tribes were later overrun by American troops.

Sitting Bull fled to Canada but returned to the United States in 1881 after he was offered amnesty. He was imprisoned for two years, then released to a reservation. In 1885, Sitting Bull was allowed to tour with Buffalo Bill's Wild West show.

There is much controversy over Sitting Bull's involvement with the rise of the ghost dance among the Lakota, a ritual that made the tribe restless during the late 1880s. Worried over a new uprising, the army ordered Sitting Bull's arrest. The chief was apprehended on December 15, 1890. As he was being led away, a scuffle ensued and shots were fired. Sitting Bull and 12 others were killed.

Sitting Bull

The visitor center at Big Hole sits overlooking the battle-field, where Nez Perce men, women, and children met and fought the soldiers of the 7th U.S. Infantry, led by Colonel John Gibbon, and 34 men of the Bitterroot Volunteers.

BIG HOLE

A GALLANT STRUGGLE

THE EXPANSION

The Nez Perce (mistakenly dubbed "pierced nose" by French explorers) tribe lived in the area where Washington, Oregon, and Idaho meet. They had voluntarily signed a peace treaty with the United States in 1855, but when gold was discovered on their land, it led to pressure to decrease the size of their reservation. The tribe split when several bands refused a new treaty.

After some warriors out for revenge attacked nearby white settlers in June 1877, the army sent in troops, which were repelled at White Bird Canyon on June 17. The nontreaty Nez Perce then began an epic trek that led pursuing soldiers on a 1,300-mile journey winding through Idaho, Montana, and Wyoming.

One of the major engagements in this epic took place on August 9, when Colonel John Gibbon's troops intercepted the Nez Perce in the Big Hole Valley. A warrior checking his horses spotted approaching soldiers and fighting started before Gibbon was ready. Although the soldiers managed

Chief Joseph

to occupy part of the camp, accurate firing from the braves forced Gibbon to retreat across the river to a pine-covered hill. As the men dug in, soldiers rolled a 12-pounder mountain howitzer into position to blast the village, but only managed to fire two rounds before a mounted charge by the Nez Perce captured and destroyed the cannon.

While the soldiers remained pinned down, the tribe gathered their belongings and headed away from the fighting. They had lost perhaps 90 men, women, and children, while army casualties were 29 killed and 40 wounded. Led by Chief Joseph, the Nez Perce headed for Canada. In late September, when only 40 miles from safety, they were attacked by troops under Colonel Nelson A. Miles, and after five days of fighting, Chief Joseph surrendered. Nearly 800 Nez Perce had started the journey; only 431 remained. The rest had been killed or had escaped. But the survivors were weary. Chief Joseph reportedly said to Miles, "From where the sun now stands, I will fight no more forever."

VISITOR INFORMATION

Name Big Hole

Classification National Battlefield

Established as a National Monument June 23, 1910; redesignated as a National Battlefield May 17, 1963

Contact P.O. Box 237, Wisdom, MT 59761

Phone 406-689-3155

Website www.nps.gov/biho

Acreage 655 (all Federal)

Points of Focus Bear Paw Battlefield Monument, Howitzer Capture Site, Nez Perce Camp Site, Nez Perce (Nee-Me-Poo) National Historic Trail, Overlook

Tours/Paths 1.2-mile Nez Perce Camp Trail, 1-mile Siege Trail

Hours Summer: 8:00 A.M. to 5:00 P.M.; winter: 9:00 A.M. to 5:00 P.M. Closed Thanksgiving, December 25, and January 1

Park Fee Individuals: $3; families of two or more: $5. Fees collected May 24 to September 21

Programs Ranger-guided tours, 12-minute orientation film, Junior Ranger program

Facilities Visitor center, picnic area, bookstore

Big Hole Valley

Captain William J. Hardee of the U.S. Army designed this black felt hat as the army's regulation dress hat. The blue hat cord and brass bugle together signify the infantry branch of service. During the Civil War, Hardee became a general in the Confederate Army.

THE CIVIL WAR

1861—1865

The seeds of civil war were sown by the U.S. Constitution, which recognized the existence of slavery and declared that five African Americans were equal to three white Americans for the purposes of representation in Congress. Throughout the first half of the nineteenth century, Northern states abolished slavery after abolitionist groups actively campaigned against the institution, using tactics such as the Underground Railroad to hide escaped slaves and openly defend escapees from pursuers who claimed their rights under the various fugitive slave laws enacted by Congress.

Civil War Union identification tag

THE LAST VETERAN

Walter Williams died on December 19, 1959. He claimed that he had served during the Civil War in a Texas regiment, and the nation mourned when he was laid to rest as the last survivor of the war. But research in pension records has shown that Walter Williams was not born until 1855 and could not possibly have served in the war. During the Great Depression, many aged men lacking money invented bogus stories of military service that were not investigated fully.

Recent research has shown that the last Confederate survivor was Pleasant Crump of the 10th Alabama, who died on December 31, 1951. The last bona fide survivor of the war was Albert Woolson, a drummer boy in the 1st Minnesota Heavy Artillery, who died on August 2, 1956. The Grand Army of the Republic erected a statue of Woolson at Gettysburg; a replica stands in Duluth, Minnesota, the soldier's postwar home.

Albert Woolson, the last legitimate veteran

"Though we fought beneath a scorching sun as well as scorching fire from the Confederates, the great Seven Days' fight is over, pictured in my mind as a terrible thunderstorm, with a goodly sprinkling of hail."

—Bates Alexander, 7th Pennsylvania Reserves

By the 1850s, North and South had begun to drift apart. The North was undergoing rapid industrialization, owing to new scientific advancements, while the South remained primarily agricultural, producing tobacco, cotton, pork, and other crops. Attacks from Northerners on the slave system met vigorous defenses by its advocates. This in turn resulted in exaggerated and often inaccurate views being held by the opposing sides about the other. Harriet Beecher Stowe's book *Uncle Tom's Cabin* further inflamed passions about the slave system.

Harriet Beecher Stowe, author of Uncle Tom's Cabin

Passions ignited by slavery extended to politics. Southern congressmen passionately defended their own interests and at times came to blows with Northerners in the Capitol. South Carolina representative Preston Brooks's physical attack on Massachusetts senator Charles Sumner typified the rancor. The birth of the Republican Party in 1856 further exacerbated sectional rivalries. Having replaced the declining Whig Party, Republicans vigorously attacked slavery and advocated its eventual abolition.

Republicans wanted to limit slavery by preventing its expansion into western territories. This stance led to a de facto civil war in the Kansas Territory in 1854 as partisans of both sides flocked to the area, stuffed ballot boxes, armed themselves, and attacked their enemies. In 1859 abolitionist John Brown led an attack on the Federal arsenal at Harper's Ferry, Virginia. Brown wanted to use weapons stored there to arm slaves and incite a widespread rebellion. But his raid failed and Brown was hanged later that year.

These events presaged a presidential campaign in 1860 that was a watershed for the future of the nation. The Republicans chose Abraham Lincoln, an Illinois lawyer, as their candidate. Democrats could not agree and the party split into sectional wings; Northerners chose Stephen A. Douglas of Illinois and Southerners opted for John C. Breckinridge of Kentucky. Those disgusted with both sides formed the Constitutional Union Party, which ran John Bell of Tennessee as its candidate. When the results were tallied, Lincoln, with only 40 percent of the popular vote, had received enough electoral votes to win the election. The other three candidates split the popular vote and made a Republican victory possible.

As a result of Lincoln's victory, South Carolinians declared that their state would leave the Union and form

John Brown

The Harper's Ferry Insurrection, 1859

THE CIVIL WAR?

The name for the war in America that took place from 1861 to 1865 has been the subject of controversy ever since the guns stopped firing. Officially, the United States government called it the War of the Rebellion. But Southerners were apt to name it the War Between the States. Later, a compromise was reached when it was termed the Civil War. But partisans of both sides still have their own names for it—the War of Northern Aggression, the War of Southern Independence, the War for the Union, and the War of Secession, among them.

CIVIL WAR CASUALTIES

Outdated battle tactics, modern weaponry, and widespread diseases combined to make the Civil War the bloodiest war in our nation's history. Deaths included 365,026 men in blue and perhaps 258,000 Confederates, a total of more than 623,000 soldiers. This total alone equals deaths in all American wars from the Revolution to Korea. A summary of American casualties:

Revolution	4,435*
War of 1812	2,260*
Mexican War	13,283
Civil War	623,026
Spanish-American War	2,446
World War I	116,708
World War II	407,316
Korean War	54,246
Vietnam War	57,685
Gulf War	269

*Total deaths are unknown; these figures represent only those killed in battle.

its own government to keep slavery safe. By the time Lincoln was sworn in as the nation's sixteenth president on March 4, 1861, several more states had joined South Carolina in forming the Confederacy, with former army officer and secretary of war Jefferson Davis as president. The new nation's Constitution was essentially a copy of the original document, and safeguarded slavery.

The Confederacy asked the new administration to remove its troops from Federal property in the South, most notably from Fort Sumter, which dominated Charleston Harbor. Lincoln, however, decided to keep the fort and ordered a relief expe-

dition to bring more troops and supplies. To forestall this, Confederate batteries opened fire on the fort on April 12, 1861, triggering civil war. When Lincoln asked for 75,000 state militia to suppress the rebellion, the states of the upper South joined the Confederacy.

The resulting four years of sectional strife were pivotal in American history. More men were killed during these four years on American soil than at any other time in history. Troops still marched into battle arrayed in straight lines as in Napoleon's wars, but the advent of new weaponry meant that the old frontal assaults were suicidal, often resulting

CIVIL WAR FIRSTS

The Civil War ushered in a new era of warfare. The CSS *Hunley* **became the first submarine to sink an enemy vessel. Union artillery compelled the surrender of the brick-built Fort Pulaski in April 1862. Opposing ironclads dueled when CSS** *Virginia* **engaged USS** *Monitor* **in March 1862. Railroads and telegraphs improved communications, while the first wartime draft in the North spawned riots in New York City.**

In 1862, the federal government enacted the first income tax. The government also began printing standard paper money and in 1863 passed a National Banking Act. With southern Democrats out of Congress, progressive legislation that had been sidelined by the slavery issue came to the fore.

The 1862 Homestead Act regulated postwar westward expansion, while the Morrill Land Grant College Act provided money for states to establish public universities—Penn State and Texas A&M are just two that benefited from the transfer of western land. A transcontinental railroad bill legislated in 1862 came to fruition in 1869 with the driving of the "golden spike" at Promontory Point, Utah.

in horrendous casualties. The war saw the first sinking of a warship by a submarine, increasing use of entrenchments by defending troops, the use of railroads to move men and supplies, balloons for aerial reconnaissance, widespread use of the telegraph system to communicate more effectively, plus other new military innovations such as the Gatling gun.

Interior view of Fort Sumter

Outnumbered, the South looked for diplomatic recognition from France and England, hoping that a shortage of cotton in Europe would tip the scales in its favor. Lincoln refused to recognize the Confederacy as a separate nation, thereby forestalling quick European intervention. Lincoln fought the war to preserve the Union, but in September 1862 he announced that if the Confederacy failed to surrender by January 1, 1863, all slaves in rebellious territory would be considered free. Thus, the war became a conflict to destroy slavery, ending any Confederate hope for foreign intervention.

The war's battles were generally fought in the South as Yankee armies invaded the Confederacy. In spite of being outnumbered, outstanding southern

generals like Robert E. Lee deflected Northern armies until 1864, when the simultaneous advance strategy advocated by Ulysses S. Grant, the new Union commanding general, wore down the South and prevented its armies from reinforcing one another. The capture of Atlanta in September 1864 by General Sherman helped ensure Lincoln's reelection and hastened the end of the war. When Confederate armies surrendered in the spring of 1865, Lincoln and Grant were in agreement not to punish the rebels, rather to let them go home to start life anew, thus avoiding guerilla warfare that might threaten the peace.

But Lincoln was assassinated by southern sympathizer John Wilkes Booth at Ford's Theater only five days after Lee's surrender at

This flag decorates the front of the Presidential box at Ford's Theater.

Appomattox. Radical Republicans then dominated the new president, Andrew Johnson, and embarked on a campaign of hatred against the former rebels. The era of Reconstruction had begun, but not as Lincoln would have wanted it to happen.

Confederate submarine CSS **Hunley**

The Chicago firm of Kurz & Allison introduced many thousands of Americans to the Civil War in the 1880s, when it issued a series of stylized prints of the war's great battles. This one, left, shows the death of Major General James B. McPherson at the battle of Atlanta on July 22, 1864. In reality, McPherson and an orderly rode into an advancing Confederate battle line and the general was shot from his horse when he ignored surrender demands and tried to gallop away.

VISITOR INFORMATION

Name Fort Sumter

Classification National Monument

Established April 28, 1948

Contact 1214 Middle Street, Sullivan's Island, SC 29482

Phone 843-883-3123

Website www.nps.gov/fosu

Acreage 194.60 (all Federal)

Points of Focus Battery Huger, casements and cannons, Confederate Defender's Plaque, Liberty Square, Union Garrison Monument

Tours/Paths Boat trip to Fort Sumter

Hours Generally open from 10:00 A.M. to 4:00 P.M. with extended summer hours. Closed Thanksgiving Day, December 25, and January 1

Park Fee Adults: $12; seniors: $11; children 6–11: $6

Programs Living History programs, interpretive talks, Junior Ranger program

Facilities Fort Sumter Visitor Education Center, museum, museum shop

Thomas Sumter

FORT SUMTER

WHERE THE CIVIL WAR BEGAN

Named for Revolutionary War hero Thomas Sumter, this five-sided brick fort controlled the entrance to Charleston Harbor. Workers had started construction in 1829 by building a manmade island in the middle of the harbor entrance, but in 1860, the fort was still unfinished. Most of the bastion's armaments had never been installed and only a small work force was generally on hand in the fort.

Charleston's main base was Fort Moultrie, where Kentucky-born Major Robert Anderson commanded the tiny garrison of the harbor. South Carolina seceded from the Union in December of 1860 and immediately began agitating for removal of Federal troops from its territory. Worried over its vulnerability to a surprise attack from local militia, Anderson abandoned Fort Moultrie on the night of December 26. His men rowed over to Fort Sumter and took possession, to the chagrin and anger of the city when it saw the American flag run up the fort's flagpole the next morning. Still, war had not yet erupted, and although the situation

Palmetto flag raised over Fort Sumter after its capture by Confederates on April 13, 1861

remained tense, Anderson continued to purchase supplies from local merchants even as his tiny force of 85 officers and men struggled to mount cannons found lying in the fort. Only 75 of the 135 prescribed for the fort were on hand.

When Abraham Lincoln was sworn in as president on March 4, 1861, he was approached by southern commissioners seeking removal of Anderson's garrison. As the negotiations dragged on, Anderson began to run short of supplies after his local market was cut off. Lincoln therefore authorized a relief expedition to bring more troops and supplies to the fort. To avoid bloodshed, the president told South Carolinians of his intentions.

In answer, Confederate authorities demanded that Anderson surrender. When he refused, Confederate batteries opened fire at 4:30 in the morning of April 12, 1861. Fort Sumter's gunners began to reply after daybreak, but a shortage of men and ammunition limited Anderson's ability to engage in anything like a fair exchange of shells. Even though the Confederates expended more than

This dramatic Currier & Ives lithograph of the bombardment on April 12 and 13, 1861, exaggerates the rate of fire coming from Fort Sumter, whose guns limited their return fire to conserve ammunition.

EDMUND RUFFIN

Born into the Virginia planter aristocracy, Edmund Ruffin (1794–1865) proved a failure in higher education and in a brief stint in the military in 1812. But he was very interested in the problems of soil infertility on his plantation and spent years working on an ultimately successful method to revitalize depleted soils. After writing an account of his work, Ruffin became publisher of the *Farmers Register* and established himself as a leading student of agriculture and soil science.

As war clouds gathered, Ruffin, who once asserted that slavery was an evil that had to be eliminated, changed his opinion and denounced northern abolitionists. After South Carolina seceded from the Union, Ruffin moved to Charleston. Although he is often credited with the honor of firing the first shot against Fort Sumter on April 12, 1861, Ruffin's action was likely preceded by other cannon fire. Still, for his appearance in the fight, Ruffin was lionized throughout the South. He returned to Virginia once his home state had joined the Confederacy. After Lee surrendered, Ruffin's mental faculty quickly faded. On June 17, 1865, the aged Southerner committed suicide.

Private Edmund Ruffin

Sergeant Peter Hart returns the Fort Sumter flag to its staff after a Rebel cannonball smashed the wooden pole.

Interior of Fort Sumter during the Confederate bombardment

THE OTHER FORT

Fort Sumter was not the only fort retained by the U.S. government when southern states began to secede. Between 1829 and 1834, the government erected Fort Pickens to protect the harbor of Pensacola, Florida. After Florida seceded in January 1861, Lieutenant Adam J. Slemmer evacuated other posts in the harbor and concentrated his men in Fort Pickens. He refused repeated surrender demands. Southern senators protested to President James Buchanan, who ordered Slemmer to maintain the garrison. An uneasy truce went into effect as both sides tried hard to avoid bloodshed. Union reinforcements arrived but remained aboard ships anchored near the fort in an effort to avoid angering the Confederates.

After Lincoln became president, he sent a navy lieutenant overland through the South with secret orders to land the troops. On April 12, the same day that war began in Charleston Harbor, Union troops strengthened Fort Pickens, assuring that this vital fort would remain in Union hands. The fort today is part of the Gulf Islands National Seashore Park.

of Morris Island and had planted numerous batteries that fired on Fort Sumter. One massive 15-day bombardment blasted the fort, reducing it to rubble and leaving only a single cannon in working order. According to General P. G. T. Beauregard, "the crumbling of the masonry under the enemy's fire, converted this portion of Fort Sumter into a mass of debris and rubbish on which the enemy's powerful artillery could make but little impression."

3,400 rounds, the bombardment caused little actual damage to the brick fort. The fort's barracks caught fire and burned during the bombardment, and a number of cannons were knocked out, but the garrison had only four men wounded. After 34 hours of fighting, and even as the Union relief expedition arrived off the harbor mouth but kept out of range of enemy shells, Anderson surrendered. The garrison was accorded the honors of war and was evacuated by the waiting Union ships. During the course of ceremonial gun firing, a cannon exploded accidentally and killed private Daniel Hough, who became the first fatality of the four-year Civil War.

Fort Sumter remained in Confederate hands for the rest of the war. In the summer of 1863, Union troops began siege operations against Charleston. By early September, the Yankees had gained control

Still, Fort Sumter's garrison, aided by other shore batteries, continued to repel Union naval attacks and even an attempted amphibious assault on the fort. By December 1863, Union gunners had thrown more than 26,000 rounds of ammunition into Sumter, but the fort continued to fly the Confederate flag. The garrison was evacuated as part of a general withdrawal in February 1865, when Union soldiers from the 52nd Pennsylvania planted their regimental colors on the debris. On April 14, 1865, four years to the day after he had surrendered the fort, Anderson returned to raise the same flag he had lowered in 1861.

Fort Pickens, Pensacola Harbor, Florida

This Kurz & Allison print of First Manassas shows the rout of McDowell's Union Army. In the foreground, the dreaded Black Horse Cavalry attacks Union Zouaves as other troops cross Bull Run Bridge.

MANASSAS
TWO BATTLES AT BULL RUN

VISITOR INFORMATION

Name Manassas

Classification National Battlefield Park

Established May 10, 1940. Boundary changes: April 17, 1954; October 30, 1980; November 10, 1988

Contact 12521 Lee Highway, Manassas, VA 20109

Phone 703-361-1339

Website www.nps.gov/mana

Acreage 5,211.62 (Federal: 4,520.44; Nonfederal: 691.18)

Points of Focus 1865 Monument, Jackson Monument on Henry House Hill, New York Zouaves Monuments, Stone Bridge, The Stone House

Tours/Paths Three self-guided walking tours, 13-mile driving tour of Second Battle of Manassas, Ranger-guided walking tour (summer season only)

Hours Visitor center open daily from 8:30 a.m. to 5:00 p.m. Closed Thanksgiving Day and December 25

Park Fee $3 per three-day pass, $20 per annual pass

Programs 45-minute battle film ($3 fee)

Facilities Visitor center, Stuart's Hill Center, museum, bookstore, picnic area

When President Abraham Lincoln issued a call for 75,000 militia to suppress the southern rebellion, the troops enlisted for a period of three months. That was presumed long enough to crush the new Confederacy, but the slow pace of training and gathering troops showed the administration that three months was insufficient. In order not to waste the thousands of troops already enlisted, in April 1861, Brigadier General Irvin McDowell, commander of Federal troops around Washington, was pressured into mounting an offensive to disperse the enemy in front of him. McDowell would next march south to capture Richmond, capital of the Confederacy.

McDowell had about 35,000 men available after detaching guards for the forts being constructed around Washington. The general planned to engage 22,000 Rebels under the command of Brigadier General P. G. T. Beauregard before the enemy received reinforcements. A second Union force led by Pennsylvania militia general Robert Patterson would cross the Potomac at Harper's Ferry and advance up the Shenandoah Valley toward Winchester, then being defended by 12,000 Confederates under the command of General Joseph E. Johnston.

McDowell's troops left Washington on July 16 and moved forward to Bull Run, a small stream that crossed the front of Beauregard's troops. After reconnoitering the area, McDowell decided to send a column upstream to outflank the rebels rather than attacking across the creek. However, unknown to McDowell, General Johnston had already arrived and was followed by the first contingents of his troops from Winchester. Patterson had moved slowly and Johnston began sending his troops by train to Manassas Junction, a short march from Bull Run.

McDowell's flanking column set out before dawn on July 21. The brigades crossed Bull Run and struck the Confederate left flank, driving the defenders slowly back. But Confederate signalmen had detected the Union maneuver and Beauregard

Ruins of Mrs. Judith Henry's house, the only civilian casualty during the battle

General Irvin McDowell

WILMER McLEAN

Wilmer McLean was an average farmer living in northern Virginia when the Civil War erupted in 1861. His farmhouse was used by Confederate general P. G. T. Beauregard as headquarters when the Confederate army assembled near Bull Run to confront the Union advance from Washington. During the battle of First Manassas, a Union artillery projectile hit the kitchen, reputedly as dinner was being cooked. His farm disrupted by the war, McLean moved his family far to the southwest to the little village of Appomattox Court House, where he bought a house and continued his work as a sugar speculator until April 1865.

When General Lee decided to discuss surrender terms with Grant, McLean offered the use of his spacious two-story brick house. It was in McLean's parlor that Grant and Lee signed the surrender terms that ended the war in Virginia. But then McLean saw his parlor ruined by souvenir seekers. General Custer bought a wooden stand and presented it as a gift to General Sheridan's wife. Other officers simply walked off with souvenirs. Even the trees outside the house were whittled away by Union soldiers anxious for something to take home. McLean later sold the house and returned to the Manassas area.

After Grant's reelection as president in 1872 McLean worked as a government employee until his death in 1882. The current McLean House in the park at Appomattox is a reconstruction of the original.

Confederate fortifications, Manassas, Virginia, March 1862

began shifting the majority of his army to face the oncoming Yankees. By noon, Union troops attacking along the front had put enough pressure on the southerners to cause their lines to waver and retreat. As Rebels fell back across the broad plateau of Henry House Hill, General Thomas J. Jackson's brigade of Virginians waited in reserve to face the Yankees. Noticing Jackson sitting calmly on his horse, General Bernard E. Bee called to his retreating troops, "Look! There stands Jackson like a stone wall! Rally behind the Virginians!" Thus was born one of the war's most famous nicknames.

Federal regiments repeatedly attacked Jackson's position only to be thrown back by the defenders. More southern troops arrived on the battlefield, some having just arrived by train from Winchester. Both sides were tired from fighting in the hot July sun that afternoon. When the 53rd Virginia, clothed in blue uniforms, fired a destructive volley into massed Federal artillery, the Union attacks finally began to falter. Southern reinforcements began to

advance, and McDowell ordered a retreat. When a southern shell crashed into a wagon that overturned on the Cub Run bridge, the retreat began to degenerate into a rout as tired and dispirited Yankees threw away their equipment, broke ranks, and ran. Rumors of Confederate cavalry in pursuit hastened the disorganized retreat to Washington. During the panic, civilians from Washington who had come to the front to see the battle were scooped up as prisoners, including one congressman. But the Confederates were too disorganized to pursue. Casualties totaled some 2,896 for McDowell and 1,982 for the Confederates, who had won the first important battle of the war.

A year later, Manassas was the scene of another encounter between blue and gray. After Major General George B. McClellan's failure to capture Richmond, the War Department united the scattered Union forces in and around Washington and the Shenandoah Valley as the Army of Virginia. Major General John Pope, fresh from victories in the Mississippi Valley, was placed in command. General Robert E. Lee detached Stonewall Jackson's corps to counter any move Pope might make. On August 9, Jackson engaged one of Pope's corps in battle at Cedar Mountain, south of Culpeper.

Once Lee received news that McClellan's troops were being evacuated from the Peninsula and sent north to reinforce Pope, he decided that Pope must

> "... at the spot where my company fought I counted where **20** balls had struck a white oak not much larger than a man's body, and nearly all within six feet of the ground. Not a bush had been missed. . . . It seems marvelous how many of us escaped being killed."
>
> —*Captain Walter W. Lenoir, 37th North Carolina*

be attacked and defeated before the two Union armies united their strength. So General James Longstreet's corps was also sent to join Jackson. While Longstreet advanced, Jackson proposed to Lee that he would circle around behind Pope's army, interdict his supplies, and force Pope to either fight at a disadvantage or retreat to Washington. The result was the campaign of Second Manassas.

Jackson's corps began to march around Pope's right flank on August 25. Two days later, the Confederates swooped down on Pope's supply base at Manassas Junction, burning whatever they could not carry away. Pope misused his mounted troops and sent his infantry searching for the elusive Confederates, who took position in an unfinished railroad bed adjoining the old Manassas battlefield. Once Jackson received word that Longstreet was marching to join him, he attacked some of Pope's troops at Brawner's Farm early in the evening of August 28.

Alerted to Jackson's whereabouts, Pope began to collect his army and during the day on August 29 hurled his troops in a series of uncoordinated assaults on Jackson's strong position. Although outnumbered and faced with defeat if the Federals were to break through, Jackson's men grimly hung on. Late in the day, Longstreet's troops began to form on Jackson's right flank. Union probing attacks revealed the presence of more Confederates, but Pope refused to believe the reports. He firmly maintained that Jackson had been beaten and was preparing to withdraw. Pope's orders for August 30 called for a pursuit of Jackson's men; even though his generals tried to advise him of the true state of affairs, Pope disbelieved them. As a result, his attacks were again repelled and later in the afternoon, Lee unleashed Longstreet's corps in a decisive attack against Pope's left flank.

Longstreet's charge drove in Pope's left and forced the Yankees to call in reinforcements to blunt the force of the attack even as Pope's troops began a retreat to Washington. The two-day battle of Second Manassas was followed by a sharp encounter at Chantilly on September 1 as Jackson tried to cut into the retreating Union columns, but was repulsed. The battles cost Pope 16,054 casualties as opposed to a loss of 9,197 southern troops, and Pope's retreat paved the way for Lee's invasion of Maryland.

Dedication of the Manassas Battle Monument

General John Pope

VISITOR INFORMATION

Name Wilson's Creek

Classification National Battlefield

Established April 22, 1960; redesignated December 16, 1970

Contact 6424 W. Farm Road 182, Republic, MO 65738

Phone 417-732-2662

Website www.nps.gov/wicr

Acreage 1,749.91 (all Federal)

Points of Focus Bloody Hill, Gibson's Mill, Guibor's Battery, Price's Headquarters, Pulaski Arkansas Battery, Ray House and Cornfield, Siegel's Final Position, Siegel's Second Position

Tours/Paths 5-mile self-guided driving tour, five walking trails, horseback and hiking trail system

Hours Open daily 8:00 A.M. to 5:00 P.M. Closed December 25 and January 1

Park Fee $3 per person or $5 per vehicle

Programs 13-minute orientation film, Living History programs, Junior Ranger program

Facilities Visitor center, picnic pavilion, research library, bookstore

WILSON'S CREEK
BLOODY BATTLE IN MISSOURI

Missouri was divided as the Civil War began. Although Governor Claiborne Jackson was pro-southern, a substantial German population in St. Louis and elsewhere remained staunchly loyal to the Union. Union Brigadier General Nathaniel Lyon neutralized pro-southern militia units, seized Jefferson City, then followed the fleeing governor into southwest Missouri, where General Sterling Price was assembling an army of Missourians to regain the state for the Confederacy.

By mid-July 1861, Lyon had advanced to Springfield, where he learned that he was badly outnumbered. Price had been reinforced by Arkansas and Louisiana troops; his army now numbered about 12,000 men. Undaunted, Lyon decided to attack. Leaving a thousand men to guard his supplies, Lyon detached Colonel Franz Sigel and his brigade of 1,200 men to circle behind Price's encampments along Wilson's Creek, 10 miles southwest of Springfield. Lyon planned to launch a frontal assault with 4,300 men, hoping to surprise and panic Price's raw recruits.

On the morning of August 10, Lyon's force emerged from the morning mist to rout the troops in Price's first encampments. Lyon's column forged ahead and occupied the crest of a low ridge before grinding to a halt when Confederate artillery opened fire. Meanwhile, upon hearing the noise of Lyon's attack, Sigel opened fire on unsuspecting Confederates in camps in front of him. After some initial success, Sigel mistakenly allowed an enemy unit to approach close to his line and fire a volley. His men abandoned their artillery and fled.

Sigel's failure allowed the Confederates to concentrate their efforts on Lyon's troops. The fighting on the ridge, nicknamed Bloody Hill by the combatants, was obstinate and fierce. Lyon's men repelled three attacks before Lyon, already twice wounded, was killed. Major Samuel D. Sturgis then authorized a withdrawal, his men being outnumbered and short on ammunition. Price did not pursue. Casualties totaled 1,317 for the Federals and 1,222 for the Confederates. While Wilson's Creek was a tactical Confederate victory, Lyon's bold gamble delayed Confederate plans and in the long run helped secure Missouri for the Union.

General Lyon leads his men into battle.

Union Brigadier General Nathaniel Lyon is mortally wounded by Confederate rifle fire during the Battle of Wilson's Creek, Missouri. Samuel D. Sturgis, replacing Lyon, ordered a retreat to Springfield. The Confederates were unable to follow up this tactical victory, allowing the Union to maintain control of southwestern Missouri.

A scene from the Battle of Fort Donelson shows Union soldiers assembling an overly stylized fort. Indecision on the part of the Confederate generals allowed Grant to drive them back into the fort and force a mass surrender.

FORT DONELSON

UNCONDITIONAL SURRENDER

VISITOR INFORMATION

Name Fort Donelson

Classification National Battlefield

Established Park—March 26, 1928. Cemetery—Union soldiers reinterred in 1867. Transferred from War Department August 10, 1933

Contact P.O. Box 434, Dover, TN 37058

Phone 931-232-5348

Website www.nps.gov/fodo

Acreage Park—551.69 (Federal: 539.89; Nonfederal: 11.80). Cemetery—15.34 (all Federal)

Points of Focus Confederate Monument, Dover Hotel, Forge Road, French Battery, Jackson's Battery, Log Huts, National Cemetery, River Batteries

Tours/Paths 5.7 miles of hiking trails, self-guided walking tour

Hours Visitor center open daily from 8:00 A.M. to 5:00 P.M. Closed December 25. Surrender House open from June to September, 12:00 P.M. to 4:00 P.M.

Park Fee Free

Programs Audiovisual introductory program, Junior Ranger program

Facilities Visitor center, museum, bookstore, campsite

In February 1862, the Union high command approved a joint army-navy attack on Forts Henry and Donelson, two southern earthwork forts that controlled traffic on the Tennessee and Cumberland Rivers. General Ulysses S. Grant was in command of the army troops while Flag Officer Andrew H. Foote led a flotilla of four ironclads and two wooden gunboats. Fort Henry fell to the Union navy on February 6.

Grant's men were in position to attack Fort Donelson on February 13. His 15,000 soldiers were opposed by approximately 20,000 southerners under the command of General John B. Floyd, a former U.S. Secretary of War from Virginia. Foote's armored ships attacked on February 13, but his slow-moving vessels were repeatedly hit by shells and forced to retreat. Foote himself was badly wounded and later died from his injuries.

In the meantime Grant had almost surrounded the Confederate earthworks with his troops. Floyd was determined to break out and retreat to avoid a siege. The Rebels attacked Grant's right flank early

Fort Donelson water battery

on the morning of February 15 and were initially successful. But then indecision and delay on Floyd's part gave Grant the opportunity to bring up more troops, counterattack, and drive the enemy back into their fortifications.

That night Floyd decided to abandon his command; he placed his Virginia regiments on transport vessels and steamed away. He was afraid that if captured he might be tried for treason. His second in command, General Gideon J. Pillow, followed suit and turned command of the fort over to General Simon B. Buckner, a Kentuckian who had joined the Confederacy.

That evening more Yankee reinforcements arrived, giving Grant 27,000 soldiers. On the sixteenth, Buckner hoisted a white flag and asked for terms. "No terms except unconditional and immediate surrender can be accepted," replied Grant. Buckner accepted, and 15,000 Confederates were taken prisoner. The press quickly nicknamed the Union general "Unconditional Surrender Grant," whose twin victories had forced a Confederate withdrawal from most of Tennessee.

Flag Officer Andrew H. Foote

VISITOR INFORMATION

Name Pea Ridge

Classification National Military Park

Established July 20, 1956

Contact P.O. Box 700, Pea Ridge, AR 72751

Phone 479-451-8122

Website www.nps.gov/peri

Acreage 4,300.35 (Federal: 4,278.75; Nonfederal: 21.60)

Points of Focus Elkhorn Tavern, Leetown Battlefield, Pratt's Store, Telegraph/Military Road, West Overlook

Tours/Paths 7-mile self-guided driving tour, hiking trails, and horse trails

Hours Open daily from 8:00 A.M. to 5:00 P.M. Closed Thanksgiving Day, December 25, and January 1

Park Fee $3 per person; $5 maximum per vehicle, $15 individual annual pass

Programs 28-minute orientation film, Junior Ranger program

Facilities Visitor center, museum, picnic area, recreational park (requires additional entry fee)

General Samuel R. Curtis

PEA RIDGE
MISSOURI SAVED FOR THE UNION

After the Union defeat at Wilson's Creek, Missouri, in August 1861, General Samuel R. Curtis took command and embarked on an offensive in February 1862. His troops maneuvered Sterling Price's men out of Missouri into northwestern Arkansas before the Confederate government sent Benjamin McCulloch's troops to reinforce Price. But these two commanders bickered with each other, and the aggressive General Earl Van Dorn was placed in command of the joint army, which included 1,000 Native Americans.

Van Dorn decided to counter Curtis's offensive with his own. He outnumbered Curtis slightly: 14,000 to 11,000. Curtis took position behind Little Sugar Creek, his men building earthworks to defend the creek. Behind them lay the high ground known as Pea Ridge.

Rather than assail Curtis's strong position, Van Dorn embarked on a bold plan. He divided his army in half and sent Price's Missourians on a march behind Pea Ridge to Elkhorn Tavern, where his men might block Curtis's retreat route. Meanwhile, McCulloch's troops would attack the Union right flank from the direction of Leetown, a small village south of Pea Ridge. Threatened to his right and rear, Curtis would have to withdraw or be annihilated.

Curtis was soon aware of Van Dorn's movements and reacted swiftly. On March 7, 1862, one of his divisions went to Elkhorn Tavern and fought Price's troops to a standstill while his other units engaged McCulloch's column. McCulloch was killed during the confused fighting and the roar of Yankee artillery discouraged his Native American allies. After dark, McCulloch's survivors moved to Elkhorn Tavern, where they joined Price's men. Van Dorn decided against retreat and hoped to confront Curtis again on March 8.

Curtis obliged Van Dorn by attacking after his artillery silenced their counterparts, and on March 9, Van Dorn ordered a retreat. Curtis suffered a loss of 1,384 and Van Dorn more than 2,000 in the two-day Battle of Pea Ridge, also known as Elkhorn Tavern. But Van Dorn's retreat meant that Missouri was safe from invasion for the foreseeable future.

Reconstructed Elkhorn Tavern

Kurz & Allison capture essential elements of the Pea Ridge battle in this lithograph. Union artillery was instrumental in this fight, discouraging Price's Native American units and paving the way for Curtis's success on the second day of the battle.

19

UNKNOWN.

Thousands of graves of Civil War soldiers are simply marked as "Unknown." The army issued no dog tags, and many soldiers carried no identification. When slain in battle, many men were buried near where they fell and often moved years later to proper cemeteries.

SHILOH
THE WAR'S FIRST BLOODBATH

VISITOR INFORMATION

Name Shiloh

Classification National Military Park

Established Park—December 27, 1894. Transferred from War Department August 10, 1933. Boundary changes; June 25, 1947; August 11, 1957; May 16, 1958. Cemetery—1866. Transferred from War Department August 10, 1933

Contact 1055 Pittsburg Landing Road, Shiloh, TN 38376

Phone 731-689-5696

Website www.nps.gov/shil

Acreage Park—3,996.64 (Federal: 3,941.64; Nonfederal: 55.00). Cemetery—10.05 (all Federal)

Points of Focus Bloody Pond, Grant's Last Line, General Albert Sidney Johnston Monument, Hornet's Nest, The Peach Orchard, Pittsburgh Landing, Ruggles' Battery, Shiloh Church

Tours/Paths 10-mile self-guided driving tour, hiking trails

Hours Open daily from 8:00 A.M. to 5:00 P.M. Closed Thanksgiving, December 25, and January 1

Park Fee $3 per person; $5 maximum per vehicle, $15 individual annual pass

Programs 25-minute orientation film, Ranger-led programs (summer season only), Junior Ranger program

Facilities Visitor center, bookstore, picnic area

After the capture of Forts Henry and Donelson in February 1862, Brigadier General Ulysses S. Grant's Federal troops, named the Army of the Tennessee, moved up the Tennessee River to a place called Pittsburgh Landing, barely 23 miles from Corinth, Mississippi, the main Confederate supply base. Grant's successful campaign had unhinged the Confederate defensive line for Kentucky and Tennessee. Rebel troops retreated south to Corinth even as Union general Don Carlos Buell's troops marched into Nashville. Major General Henry W. Halleck, in command of Union troops west of the Appalachian Mountains, ordered Grant to remain at Pittsburgh Landing until Buell moved to join him. Then the combined armies would seize Corinth.

Confederate general Albert Sidney Johnston was in charge of the Rebel troops opposing Grant. He

General Ulysses S. Grant rallying his troops during the Battle of Shiloh

assembled 40,000 men at Corinth, organized them as the Army of the Mississippi, and moved north to attack Grant before Buell's troops reached the area. Johnston realized that if Buell arrived first, he would be badly outnumbered and unable to resist the combined Union armies.

Johnston's advance troops neared the Union lines on April 5. Union pickets quickly realized the enemy was in the woods in front of their camps and reported their discovery. However, Grant's subordinates discounted these reports, which they felt were the exaggerated imaginings of inexperienced soldiers.

Johnston ordered an advance early on the morning of Sunday, April 6. The initial Confederate assaults by William J. Hardee's corps struck the Yankee encampments of divisions led by William T. Sherman and Benjamin M. Prentiss. Some men in blue were literally caught with their pants down as

Major General Henry W. Halleck

AN ARMY COMMANDER'S STRANGE DEATH

Albert Sidney Johnston directed the Confederate attack on Grant's camps at Shiloh. Later that day, the general witnessed repeated Confederate attacks against the Union defenders of the "Hornet's Nest" area of the battlefield. Sometime during the fighting, Johnston was hit by a minié ball in the back of his right leg. Johnston had suffered a wound during a duel in 1837 and his right leg was generally numb to heat, cold, and pain. Tennessee governor Isham Harris, one of Johnston's aides, had just returned from a mission when the general reeled in the saddle. Harris helped Johnston to the ground and sent for his physician, who had left to help tend wounded men of both armies. Harris was unable to find a wound except for the gunshot wound in Johnston's leg, which was easily treatable if quickly located. But Johnston must have been shot minutes earlier and his knee-high boot had filled with blood, which he seemingly did not notice in the heat of combat. Johnston soon died from an acute loss of blood; the bullet had severed an artery and he bled to death. Ironically, a tourniquet was found in his coat pocket. If used properly, it would have saved his life.

General A. S. Johnston

"The battle now raged with indescribable fury. . . the roar of the artillery, and the incessant rattle of the small arms."

—*Peter W. Alexander, correspondent for the* Savannah Republican, *April 18, 1862*

Confederates achieved surprise in their initial attacks. The forward Union camps were captured as their occupants alternately fled, rallied, and retreated under enemy pressure.

By 10:30 A.M., Prentiss had managed to rally much of his division and took position along an old wagon road about a mile to the rear. Other units formed on his flanks as Yankees continued to retreat to a series of high bluffs overlooking Pittsburgh Landing. Grant, headquartered on a troop transport, had arrived and was endeavoring to form a defensive line as a last stand. But the Confederates were as much disorganized by victory as the Yanks were by defeat. The wooded terrain had disrupted lines of battle, and many starved southerners had fallen out of line to pillage the abandoned Union camps.

However, shortly after noon, Braxton Bragg's Confederate troops began the first of a series of attacks on Prentiss's position. After two hours of piecemeal attacks, Prentiss still held his ground, but he was in danger of being cut off from Grant's still-forming line in his rear. The action centered on what soldiers called the "Hornet's Nest," where the fighting was protracted and bloody.

Recapture of artillery by a portion of General Lovell H. Rosseau's command on April 7, 1862

General Johnston personally was in the fray here, encouraging his men and sending in reinforcements. But the general was shot in his right leg as he led men into battle. He dismissed the injury at first, but then bled to death because the bullet had severed a vital artery. General P. G. T. Beauregard then assumed command of the Confederate army.

By six o'clock, continued Rebel assaults finally overwhelmed Prentiss, who surrendered with the remnants of his division. But his holding action of five hours delayed active Confederate attacks elsewhere, enabling Grant to deploy artillery batteries and rally the other divisions. Two Union wooden gunboats, *Lexington* and *Tyler*, also arrived and threw shells into the Confederate lines. At dusk, Beauregard sent in an attack on the new line, which repelled the southerners. The enemy then withdrew to rest and prepare to continue the battle the next day.

That night, however, Lew Wallace's division arrived on the battlefield and four of Buell's divisions were ferried across the river to join Grant's survivors. At dawn on April 7, Grant and Buell sent their troops forward to recapture lost ground. The relentless Union attack rolled forward and drove back

General Benjamin M. Prentiss (mounted) directs the fighting at Hornet's Nest.

Beauregard's tired men. Sometime around 3:30, Beauregard ordered a retreat. Many of his regiments were out of ammunition and his troops were now badly outnumbered by the combined Union armies. The Yankees failed to pursue the Rebels. Cavalry led by Nathan Bedford Forest skillfully covered the retreat, which was hampered by a heavy overnight rain.

This Battle of Shiloh, so named for a small log meeting house on the battlefield, was shocking news to families across the divided country. Grant's losses totaled 13,047, while the Confederates counted 10,699 casualties. The bloodbath at Shiloh was only a precursor of bat-tles to come, but its severity and long casualty lists appalled both sides. Critics of Lincoln's adminis-tration called for Lincoln to fire Grant.

Newspapers reported that the general had been drunk and mishandled the fighting. In response, Lincoln reputedly asked what brand of whiskey Grant used; he wished to send some to those of his generals who refused to fight.

In the end, Halleck personally came to the front and took command, relegating Grant to a subordi-nate role as second in command. The cautious Halleck brought in more troops and in early May began a slow movement toward Corinth. Worried about surprise attacks, the general ordered earth-works erected every night to protect his camps. By May 25, his men had finally approached the Corinth defenses. Beauregard, outnumbered more than two to one, evacuated the city and retreated. Corinth was occupied by Halleck's troops on May 30 and remained in Union hands for the rest of the war.

Lewis Wallace

FORT PULASKI

THE END OF BRICK FORTS

Named for Revolutionary War hero Count Casimir Pulaski, this five-sided brick fort guarded the water approaches to the Georgia port city of Savannah. Located on Cockspur Island at the mouth of the Savannah River, Fort Pulaski's defenses would repel any seaborne attack against Savannah. The fort, with its 7½-foot-thick brick walls, had been constructed between 1829 and 1847 at a cost of over a million dollars.

When Georgia seceded from the Union in 1861, militia seized the fort and quickly brought it up to battle readiness, mounting 48 of a possible 140 cannons that could be positioned inside the bastion. Colonel Charles H. Olmstead, in command of the 1st Georgia regiment, was placed in charge of defending the fort.

In November 1861, a Union army–navy expedition attacked and captured the Confederate forts guarding Hilton Head, South Carolina, placing the Yankees within striking distance of Fort Pulaski. Union general Quincy A. Gillmore planned to capture the fort. His infantry occupied Tybee Island and installed 26 smoothbores and 10 newer rifled pieces such as 30-pounder Parrotts. Union batteries were located from 1,650 to 3,400 yards from the fort. When his batteries were ready, Gillmore sent a flag of truce to Colonel Olmstead; demanding a surrender to avoid bloodshed. "I am here to defend the fort, not to surrender it," was Olmstead's heroic reply.

Thus, Gillmore's cannons opened fire on the morning of April 10, 1862. Bolts from the Parrotts gouged holes in Pulaski's walls as they tore large sections of bricks loose. After a 30-hour bombardment, Olmstead hoisted a white flag and surrendered the bastion. Union artillery had fired more than 5,200 projectiles at the fort, seriously damaging its walls and placing the interior powder magazines in jeopardy if struck. Remarkably, only one Confederate soldier was killed and a handful wounded during the intense bombardment.

Once captured, Fort Pulaski remained in Union hands throughout the war, effectively closing Savannah to blockade running. Rifled cannon projectiles could wear down and breach brick walls with relative ease, making these old forts obsolete.

Bombardment of Fort Pulaski, Cockspur Island, Georgia

The walls of Fort Pulaski that faced Union bombardment suffered heavy damage. This view shows the interior at one of the casements in the fort's lower tier of guns. Rubble from the blasted wall made this gun all but useless. Union soldiers later repaired most of the damage, and the fort remained a key Federal position.

Union troops under Brigadier General Silas Casey's command built this earthen redoubt in May 1862. Attacking Confederate troops overran this position after heavy fighting during the Battle of Fair Oaks. The twin farmhouses in the background were a prominent feature on this part of the battlefield. (Today, this area is the site of a housing development.)

RICHMOND

BELEAGUERED CONFEDERATE CAPITAL

VISITOR INFORMATION

Name Richmond

Classification National Battlefield Park

Established March 2, 1936. Boundary change: March 3, 1956

Contact 3215 East Broad Street, Richmond, VA 23223

Phone 806-226-1981

Website www.nps.gov/rich

Acreage 7,307.00 (Federal: 773.03; Nonfederal: 6,533.97)

Points of Focus Beaver Dam Creek, Chickahominy Bluff, Cold Harbor, Drewry's Bluff, Fort Harrison, Gaines' Mill, Malvern Hill, Parker's Battery, Tredegar Iron Works, Watt House

Tours/Paths Self-guided walking tours, driving tour

Hours Open daily 9:00 A.M. to 5:00 P.M. Closed Thanksgiving, December 25, and January 1

Park Fee Free

Programs Orientation film, Junior Ranger program, several special events throughout the year

Facilities Chimborazo Medical Museum, five visitor centers, picnic area

When the Confederate government voted to move its capital to Richmond, Virginia, in May 1861, it meant that this city would become a focal point of contending armies. A hundred miles from Washington, Richmond was the state's major city and cultural center, situated at the head of navigation along the James River. The city also contained the Tredegar Iron Works, one of the South's largest such industries, as well as several other important businesses.

Major General George B. McClellan, in command of the Union Army of the Potomac, planned a major campaign designed to capture the city and end the war in the spring of 1862. Rather than advance overland, his massive 120,000-man force landed at Fort Monroe, at the tip of the peninsula, then approached the Yorktown defenses. Here Confederate general John B. Magruder held off the Yankees until reinforced by General Joseph E. Johnston's entire army. But still outnumbered, Johnston elected to avoid McClellan's planned siege

Siege trenches as they look today

operations and withdrew, fighting a rearguard battle at Williamsburg on May 5. A Union naval squadron attempted to approach Richmond via the James River, but on May 15 it was repelled by Confederate armaments located in Fort Darling at Drewry's Bluff.

McClellan then moved to within a few miles of Richmond, with his army on both sides of the flooded Chickahominy River. Johnston attacked the Union left at Fair Oaks (also called Seven Pines) on May 31–June 1, but after a sharp battle, Union reinforcements crossed the river and Johnston withdrew. The general himself was wounded in this battle; President Jefferson Davis replaced him with Robert E. Lee.

Subsequently Lee decided on an aggressive strategy to drive the Yankees away from Richmond. Fighting at Oak Grove on June 25 near the old Fair Oaks battlefield was a diversion to mask Lee's major attacks north of the Chickahominy, where he was attempting to destroy one of McClellan's corps, Union general Fitz John Porter's Fifth Corps. Stonewall Jackson's troops traveled by rail from the

Major General George McClellan

THE GREAT ESCAPE

Situated in Richmond near the James River front, Libby Prison was an old tobacco warehouse that became a prison for Union officers. Terrible living conditions and overcrowding quickly made it one of the most notorious prisons in the Confederacy. Many men attempted escape; the largest of such efforts was led by Colonel Thomas E. Rose. Under the watchful eye of prison guards, it took a group of prisoners a mere 17 days to dig a 53-foot-long tunnel underneath the prisons, under a street, and into a backyard nearby. On February 9, 1886, 109 officers escaped through this tunnel; 59 reached Union lines, 2 drowned, and 48 were re-captured, including Colonel Rose. In 1888, a Chicago business purchased the building, dismantled it brick by brick, numbered every piece, and reassembled the old prison in Chicago. It then opened as a museum, closing a decade later. In 1899 it was torn down to make way for developers, and pieces of the prison were either discarded or sold.

Libby Prison

Battle of Cold Harbor

Shenandoah Valley to reinforce Lee's Army of Northern Virginia. The first major engagement of the Seven Days Battles took place on June 25 when Lee's troops attacked Porter at Mechanicsville, also known as Beaver Dam Creek. Jackson failed to arrive on time and Porter's troops easily repelled Lee's frontal attacks. Porter fell back behind Boatswain's Swamp that night. Then followed the June 26 Battle of Gaines' Mill, where Porter's tired men repelled several enemy attacks. But by day's end, Longstreet and Jackson broke through and Porter fell back across the Chickahominy.

Porter's retreat influenced McClellan to change his supply base from White House on the Pamunkey River to Harrison's Landing on the James. His army destroyed what supplies it could not carry, abandoned several hospitals filled with sick and wounded men, and began a retreat toward the James River.

Lee, hoping to catch McClellan's army, which was strung out in columns, hit the Pennsylvania Reserves division at Glendale on June 30. The fighting here (also known as Frayser's Farm and New Market Crossroads) was fierce, bloody, and obstinate, but the Pennsylvania troops,

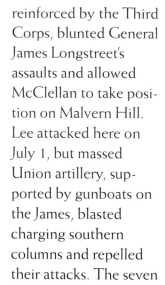

reinforced by the Third Corps, blunted General James Longstreet's assaults and allowed McClellan to take position on Malvern Hill. Lee attacked here on July 1, but massed Union artillery, supported by gunboats on the James, blasted charging southern columns and repelled their attacks. The seven days cost McClellan 15,855 casualties. Lee's army suffered a loss of 20,204, but it had driven McClellan away from Richmond.

Subsequent Union raids directed against Richmond's growing defenses failed for the next two years. In May 1864, Lieutenant General Ulysses S. Grant directed George Meade's Army of the Potomac against Lee's army in a massive campaign that began in the Wilderness and wound up in siege operations at Petersburg in mid-June. After inconclusive battles at the Wilderness, Spotsylvania, and the North Anna, the two armies converged on the crossroads of Cold Harbor, situated on part of the old Gaines' Mill battlefield of two years before. Grant had continued to attempt to outflank all of Lee's positions ever since the campaign began, and the race to Cold Harbor echoed the Union general's earlier strategy.

Reinforced by 16,000 men from General Benjamin Butler's Army of the James, Grant directed Meade to seize the crossroads and attempt to outflank Lee yet again. Even though Union cavalry grabbed the crossroads on May 31 and reinforcing infantry from the Sixth Corps solidified their position, Lee's army sidled to the left and entrenched to face the Yankees. Lee, worried about being out-flanked and knowing of Union reinforcements, wired to President Davis, expressing concern that if his own army was not augmented, he faced "disaster." Within hours, a fresh division from the Petersburg defenses moved to join Lee.

A Union frontal attack by the Sixth Corps was repelled on June 1, causing 2,200 Union casualties. Grant planned more assaults on June 2 and ordered General Winfield S. Hancock's Second Corps into position, but hot weather enervated the marching infantry and the attack was rescheduled for June 3. But three corps that assailed Lee's entrenched veterans that day were again repelled after some minor lodgements in the enemy fortifications. Grant's loss for the entire Battle of Cold Harbor totaled some 12,000 men. The general then decided to shift his troops across the James River to strike at Petersburg.

The subsequent siege operations around Petersburg occasionally involved troops that had been defending Richmond as well. Union operations on the north bank of the James centered around their bridgehead at Deep Bottom. Occasional forays against Richmond's defenses were primarily in an effort to divert Lee's attention when Union troops maneuvered on the left of the line toward Petersburg's vital railroads.

One major operation took place in late September 1864. Troops from the Army of the James moved to the New Market Heights area to assault the Richmond defenses even as Union troops moved westward from the Petersburg siege lines on the other end of the Union positions. On September 29 Confederate Fort Harrison fell to a determined Yankee assault that included black troops; 14 African Americans later were awarded Medals of Honor for their gallantry in this attack. Later attacks against Fort Gilmer failed, but Fort Harrison remained in Union hands, necessitating a realignment of the Richmond defenses to the north.

During the war, Richmond's population dramatically increased as refugees fled areas of fighting and moved into the city. The city also boasted the Confederacy's largest hospital (Chimborazo, location of the current park headquarters) and contained several POW camps, including Belle Island and Libby Prison. When Lee evacuated Petersburg on April 2, 1865, the Richmond garrison also retreated. Union troops marched into the city on April 3, helping to control fires set by retreating Rebels who burned military property.

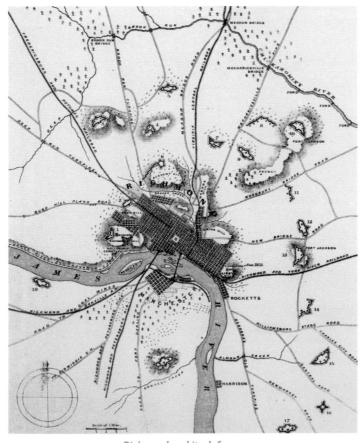

Richmond and its defenses

ZOUAVES

Named for a Berber tribe from Algeria that fought for the French, Zouaves were infantry units that adopted the colorful garb of these French units—a short dark blue jacket with yellow or red trim, baggy trousers (red or blue), a woolen sash, white leggings, and a red fez for a cap, often with a turban as well. In 1859, Elmer Ellsworth organized the United States Zouave Cadets of Chicago; his tour across the north led many militia companies to adopt a flashy Zouave uniform. When the Civil War began, several entire regiments of men clothed in various Zouave-style uniforms appeared. Perhaps the best known was the 5th New York Infantry, known as Duryee's Zouaves after its first commander. During the Battle of Gaines' Mill, the 5th New York held the right of the Union line. The Zouaves encountered a brigade of South Carolinians and inflicted heavy casualties on it. But in return, the 5th lost a third of its 450 men, including 54 killed.

Zouave uniform of the 5th New York

ANTIETAM

AMERICA'S BLOODIEST DAY

Following his conquest of John Pope at the Battle of Second Manassas, General Robert E. Lee decided to launch an offensive into Maryland. He hoped to recruit sympathetic Marylanders into his army, ease the burden on northern Virginia farmers, and perhaps win a victory on northern soil, an action that might lead to foreign recognition of the Confederacy.

Lee's army of 40,000 men began crossing the Potomac River on September 4. A Federal garrison of 12,000 soldiers at Harper's Ferry threatened Lee's communications with Virginia. Seeing that recruits were not flocking to the Stars and Bars, Lee divided his army into four separate columns, sending three under the command of Stonewall Jackson to encircle and capture Harper's Ferry. Lee remained behind with General James Longstreet in Maryland, looking for supplies and watching the roads toward Washington.

In the meantime, General George B. McClellan reassumed command of the demoralized Union armies congregated in the Washington defense perimeter. McClellan used his genius for organization and quickly had the old Army of Virginia merged into his own Army of the Potomac. After leaving behind a substantial force to protect the capital, McClellan set out with about 80,000 men in five corps to confront Lee. Confederate cavalry quickly alerted Lee to McClellan's advance, so the outnumbered Confederates pulled out of Frederick and retreated to the passes through South Mountain west of the city.

McClellan's army moved into the Frederick area on September 13. That morning Union soldiers from the 27th Indiana regiment discovered Lee's General Orders Number 191, wrapped around three cigars. A staff officer must have carelessly dropped these orders, which were passed along to McClellan. Jubilant that he had Lee's battle plans, McClellan could scarcely believe his good luck.

McClellan's troops assailed the Rebel defenders of South Mountain on September 14. This engagement, known as the Battle of South Mountain, took

Signal tower overlooking Antietam battlefield

This part of the famous Sunken Road at Antietam, now a peaceful farm lane, became a key battlefield point. Today, reconstructed wooden fences, closely mown grass, and stone monuments disguise the carnage that took place here.

CLARA BARTON

Clara Barton, a Massachusetts school-teacher, was nicknamed "the angel of the battlefield" for her humanitarian work during the Civil War. Accompanied by four teamsters and a load of provisions, Barton arrived on the battlefield the day before the epic battle at Antietam. During the battle she extracted a bullet from a soldier's cheek, helped a surgeon with amputations, and passed out her own supplies to wounded men, all while in great danger. At one point, while kneeling to tend to a soldier, a bullet whizzed past her and killed the man she was helping.

After six weeks of hard work in the hospitals, Barton became sick and returned to Washington. She worked in army hospitals sporadically during the war, and in 1865 she helped identify unknown dead at Andersonville Prison. Barton later founded the American Red Cross and was its first director. She died in 1912 at the age of 91.

Clara Barton

Kurz & Allison's lithograph of Union troops surging across Burnside's Bridge

place at Fox's and Turner's Gaps. By day's end, Union troops had driven off the defenders and were poised to relieve Harper's Ferry and also deliver a deathblow to Lee's army. But McClellan, fearing a trap, delayed his advance. As a result, Jackson seized the heights overlooking Harper's Ferry and began firing artillery into the Union lines. On September 15, Colonel Dixon S. Miles surrendered the entire garrison.

Lee retreated to the village of Sharpsburg, situated near the Potomac on a ridge overlooking Antietam Creek. Rather than retreat to Virginia, he decided to risk a battle, taking into account his adversary's usual cautious approach to fighting.

Jackson's men joined Lee, even as McClellan's right wing crossed the creek and skirmished with Jackson's troops on the evening of September 16.

The Battle of Antietam, called Sharpsburg by the Confederates, took place on September 17, which became the bloodiest day of the Civil War. McClellan outnumbered Lee by at least two to one, but instead of a concerted attack all along the line, the Union general allowed his subordinates to attack piecemeal, enabling the outnumbered Confederates to move reinforcements to threatened parts of their battle line throughout the day.

The first attacks took place shortly after dawn, when Union major general Joseph Hooker sent his

> ## "My ramrod is wrenched from my grasp as I am about to return it to its socket after loading. I look for it behind me, and the Lieutenant passes me another, pointing to my own, which lies bent and unfit for use across the face of a dead man."
>
> —*Private George Kimball, 12th Massachusetts, describing fighting in the Cornfield*

First Corps into action against the Confederate left, held by troops under Jackson's command. A 30-acre cornfield then became the center of a fierce struggle between men in blue and gray. The fighting swept to and fro across this field as the two sides charged and countercharged through almost-ripe corn. By morning's end, the field was leveled and hundreds of bodies littered its surface.

Troops from General Joseph K.F. Mansfield's Twelfth Corps relieved the battered First Corps and continued the fight, sweeping through the East Woods, across the cornfield, and into the edges of the West Woods. A small, whitewashed church used by the Dunker sect became the Union target. The church sat on a small knoll a short distance south of the cornfield, its white walls a beacon for attacking Union soldiers. But the aged General Mansfield was hit in the stomach and carried from the field soon after his men became engaged, and his corps quickly became disorganized in the swirling combat.

General Edwin V. Sumner's Second Corps then entered the fray. Sumner personally led the Second Division (led by General John Sedgwick) from Antietam Creek westward across the area of the earlier fighting into the West Woods, the men marching in three long brigade lines as if on dress parade. As the division reached the West Woods, Jackson's survivors struck from three sides; in less than 20 minutes, the Second Division disintegrated, suffering 2,300 casualties.

The rest of Sumner's corps drifted south and encountered Confederate troops under the command of D. H. Hill, arrayed in an old sunken farm lane. The Rebels repelled attack after attack until outflanked and forced to withdraw. But the defenders had mauled two Union divisions and held this portion of the line for four hours, against all odds, until flanked and driven back. Thereafter, the farm lane would be known as Bloody Lane. Conspicuous on the Union side was Thomas F. Meagher's Irish Brigade, composed largely of Irish immigrants from

Cavalry marching out of Harper's Ferry

HARPER'S FERRY

General Lee's invasion of Maryland in 1862 centered around the capture of the 12,000-man Union garrison at Harper's Ferry. Lee divided his army into four parts, sending Stonewall Jackson with three of these divisions to surround the garrison, which was under the command of Colonel Dixon S. Miles. Many of Miles's regiments were untested rookies. When Confederate troops pressured Union defensive positions, Miles evacuated the commanding Maryland Heights after only a brief engagement.

Discouraged when Confederate artillery batteries placed his men in a crossfire, Miles decided to surrender. However, Colonel Benjamin F. Davis gathered 1,300 cavalrymen, including his own 8th New York, crossed the Potomac River, and marched his horsemen along a little-used path under the very noses of Rebel sentinels to escape the trap. En route to safety, Davis happened upon General James Longstreet's reserve ammunition wagon train. His men seized and brought them as a prize into Union lines. Miles's surrender was the largest capitulation of American forces until Bataan in 1942. Miles himself was mortally wounded by an exploding shell and thus missed the court of inquiry and rebuke by the War Department over his handling of the situation.

THE YOUNGEST MEDAL OF HONOR WINNER

Bugler Johnny Cook of Battery B, 4th United States Artillery, had just turned 15 a month before going into action at Antietam. The battery unlimbered astride the Hagerstown Pike and immediately went into battle. Confederate musketry fire was heavy and the battery quickly sustained many casualties. Captain James Campbell was hit twice and his horse fell dead. Bugler Cook helped the captain to the rear and then returned to the action. He recalled: "Seeing that the cannoneers were nearly all down, and one with a pouch full of ammunition, lying dead, I unstrapped the pouch, started for the battery and worked as a cannoneer. We were then in the very vortex of battle. The enemy made three attempts to capture our guns, the last time coming within ten or fifteen feet of our guns." For his gallantry, Cook was awarded a Medal of Honor.

Johnny Cook

The Maryland State Monument, the only monument on the battlefield dedicated to the armies of both sides

New York and Boston; in spite of heavy losses, they followed their green flags into the face of murderous enemy fire. As troops moved forward in this part of the field, a Confederate shell hit some beehives on the Roulette Farmstead. A passing Pennsylvania regiment dissolved as an entire swarm of maddened bees attacked the first objects they saw—these untried Keystone State boys broke ranks and fled to avoid the stinging.

The Middle Bridge over Antietam Creek

On the southern end of the battlefield, Union general Ambrose E. Burnside was ordered to seize an arched stone bridge that spanned Antietam Creek and assail Lee's right flank. Burnside was slow in moving as he looked for a better place to cross the stream. Georgia troops occupied the heights overlooking the bridge, and their deadly fire broke up the first three Union charges against the bridge. Meanwhile, Burnside sent one of his divisions downstream to look for a ford. He also sent orders for another attack against the bridge, which came to be called Burnside's Bridge. At 1:00 P.M., two regiments charged the bridge. These men—the 51st Pennsylvania and 51st New York—reached the span together and managed to cross as the Georgians ran low on ammunition and withdrew. Burnside then crossed with his entire Ninth Corps, occupied the hills overlooking the creek, reorganized, and later in the afternoon sent his entire corps forward against Lee's out-manned right flank. Even as

Lieutenant General Ambrose P. Hill

Burnside's advance regiments reached the outskirts of Sharpsburg, troops from Ambrose P. Hill's division arrived from Harper's Ferry, racing to attack Burnside's left. This last Confederate division to reach the battlefield stemmed Burnside's advance and drove his corps back to the hills near the creek, where the blue line stabilized and held off the Confederates.

The fighting on the Union left effectively ended the day-long battle of Antietam. McClellan still had an entire corps in reserve, but the casualty rate for the day was appalling. His army had suffered 12,401 killed, wounded, and captured. Many of his regiments had just joined the army and lacked effective training; their high losses contributed to the army's butcher's bill. Lee's smaller army suffered a loss of 10,318. McClellan refused to fight the next day, and on the evening of September 18, Lee quietly slipped across the Potomac. McClellan did not pursue Lee and instead went into camp near the battlefield, causing President Lincoln great frustration.

Even though Antietam was not a clear-cut Union victory, Lincoln used it to issue a preliminary draft of his Emancipation Proclamation. If the South did not lay down its arms and return to the Union by January 1, 1863, said the president, after that date all slaves held in rebellious states would be then and forever free. Thus the Civil War became a war not only to preserve the Union but also to free the slaves.

THE 23RD OHIO AT ANTIETAM

The 23rd Ohio Volunteer Infantry was mustered into Union service during the summer of 1861. After service in western Virginia, the regiment's division was transferred temporarily to the Ninth Corps and fought in the 1862 Maryland Campaign. The regiment's commander was Rutherford B. Hayes, a Harvard Law School graduate who volunteered early in the war to help stamp out the rebellion. Hayes was a fearless combat leader; at the Battle of South Mountain on September 14, the colonel was badly wounded in the arm and was out of action for months. The commissary sergeant of the 23rd was William McKinley, only 19 years old when he participated in the Battle of Antietam. He won plaudits for his bravery under fire, when he drove his commissary wagon through a rain of shot and shell from the enemy to bring badly needed food and coffee to the regiment in battle line.

Both Hayes and McKinley entered politics after the war and used their Civil War records to good effect. Both men became president of the United States. McKinley was the last veteran of the war to be elected president. In 1903, his old unit erected a monument to his heroism on the Antietam battlefield.

Union general Ambrose E. Burnside, commanding the Army of the Potomac from his position on Stafford Heights, northeast of the Rappahannock River, issues orders to Major General Joseph Hooker during the Battle of Fredericksburg, Virginia. Hooker protested his order to assail the Confederate position on Marye's Heights overlooking Fredericksburg.

FREDERICKSBURG
EPICENTER OF VIRGINIA'S CIVIL WAR

This military park embraces fields on which men in blue and gray fought four major battles of the war, with a combined casualty list of over 100,000 officers and men. The city of Fredericksburg, situated on the Rappahannock River, lies halfway between Richmond and Washington. Although the city had been occupied briefly by Union troops in May and June 1862, the war generally had been waged elsewhere until late November 1862, when both armies moved into the area.

Union major general Ambrose E. Burnside replaced George B. McClellan as commander of the Army of the Potomac in early November. The general devised a plan by which his massive army of more than 120,000 men would sidestep Lee's Army of Northern Virginia and quickly move to Fredericksburg, where pontoon bridges would enable it to cross before Lee got there. Once across the river, Burnside would try to get between Lee and Richmond, thereby forcing a climactic battle.

But bureaucratic snafus delayed the pontoons' arrival from Washington,

Confederate statue at Fredericksburg

and by the time they arrived, Lee had guessed Burnside's maneuver and had reached the hills behind Fredericksburg and deployed his army for battle. Burnside, feeling pressure from Washington to do something before winter set in, went ahead with his plan in spite of remonstrances from his subordinates. On December 11, engineers began laying the pontoons, but Rebel sniper fire from Fredericksburg stopped them cold. Union artillery then opened fire on the city as troops rowed across the river and fought the enemy in the streets until the city was secure.

Then, with the bridges completed, Burnside's army crossed.

The Battle of Fredericksburg took place on December 13. Burnside's plan called for an attack by his left wing, but Major General William B. Franklin, in charge of that wing, interpreted his orders too literally and sent forward only George Meade's Pennsylvania Reserves division. Meade's gallant soldiers broke through Stonewall Jackson's position at Hamilton's Crossing but were repelled when reinforcements failed to exploit this gain.

On the Union right, troops under Joseph Hooker and Edwin Sumner's command marched out of the city to

VISITOR INFORMATION

Name Fredericksburg & Spotsylvania

Classification National Military Park

Established Park—February 14, 1927. Transferred from War Department August 10, 1993. Boundary changes: December 11, 1989; October 27, 1992; December 9, 1999. Cemetery—Date of Civil War interments: 1867. Transferred from War Department August 10, 1933

Contact 120 Chatham Lane, Fredericksburg, VA 22405

Phone 540-373-6122

Website www.nps.gov/frsp

Acreage Park—8,535.02 (Federal: 7,369.00; Nonfederal: 1,166.02). Cemetery—12.00 (all Federal)

Points of Focus Chancellorsville, Chatham, Fredericksburg National Cemetery, Old Salem Church, Spotsylvania Court House, Stonewall Jackson Shrine

Tours/Paths 23 miles of walking, hiking, and biking trails; self-guided driving tour

Hours Open daily from 9:00 A.M. to 5:00 P.M. Closed Thanksgiving Day, December 25, and January 1

Park Fee $4 per person; $20 per individual annual pass

Programs Junior Ranger program, Ranger-led programs (summer season only)

Facilities Two visitor centers, picnic areas

General Ambrose E. Burnside

A CONFEDERATE'S HEROISM

During the bloody Union repulses at Fredericksburg's Marye's Heights, dozens of wounded men in blue lay in front of the enemy-occupied stone wall. Sergeant Richard Kirkland of the 2nd South Carolina was so moved by their desperate cries for help that he wanted to go over the wall and give them water. Against the better judgment of his commander, Kirkland collected canteens from several comrades and slowly stood up. He cautiously jumped over the wall and went to the nearest Union man. When it was seen that he was on an errand of mercy, nobody shot at him. Kirkland was allowed to administer to all the wounded within his range; then he returned to his post. Kirkland was killed in battle later in the war.

assail southern troops on Marye's Heights. Confederate troops sheltered by a stone wall and amply supported by artillery mowed down the Union attackers, who were unable to get close to the enemy. Lee, watching the slaughter, remarked, "It is well war is so terrible. We should grow too fond of it."

The following day was spent in skirmishing as Burnside debated what to do. But that night, his army silently recrossed the river and went into winter quarters. Casualties totaled 12,653 Federals and only 5,309 Confederates. Fredericksburg was Lee's most lopsided victory of the war.

After the battle, recriminations on the Union side led to Burnside's dismissal and his replacement by Major General Joseph Hooker. Hooker instituted much-needed changes to bolster the shattered morale of his army. By the spring of 1863, the Army of the Potomac was, according to its commander, "the finest army on the planet." Hooker's plans called for a portion of his army to move northwest along the Rappahannock, then quickly cross both this river and the smaller Rapidan. This would enable his troops to move through an area called the Wilderness because of its largely wooded terrain, and approach Lee's rear flank. The rest of the army would confront

Major General Joseph "Fighting Joe" Hooker

Lee at Fredericksburg and prevent him from sending troops to oppose the flanking maneuver. Union cavalry would conduct a raid far to the rear to intercept Lee's communications. If all went well, Hooker boasted, Lee would either have to come out of his fortifications to fight, or retreat to Richmond.

The campaign began on April 13, 1863, when Union horsemen departed on their raid. Rainy weather hampered their effectiveness, and it was not until April 27 that Hooker and three of his seven infantry corps began the flanking movement. By nightfall on April 30, these corps were grouped around a mansion called Chancellorsville, situated in cleared land in the midst of the Wilderness, less than 20 miles west of Fredericksburg. An elated Hooker called for the Third and most of the Second Corps to join him, giving him a clear superiority over Lee's depleted army; Lee had sent General Longstreet with part of his corps to the Suffolk region to guard against Union raids and gather supplies, and Longstreet was still absent.

Lee nevertheless had fathomed Hooker's intentions and sent his divisions west to confront the Union general. When skirmishing erupted on the morning of May 1, Hooker, instead of sending his troops forward until they cleared the Wilderness, pulled his divisions back into a defensive position to await Lee's attack. Later that day southern cavalry discovered that Hooker's right flank was unguarded. Reacting to this news, Lee and Stonewall Jackson took a gamble. Jackson took three divisions (28,000 men), circled around to Hooker's right and attacked, leaving Lee with two divisions to oppose any sudden advance. A single division still occupied the Fredericksburg positions.

Confederate dead behind the stone wall of Marye's Heights, photographed in May 1863

Union troops build pontoon bridges across the Rappahannock River on December 12, 1862.

MUSIC UNDER FIRE

On May 6, 1864, the 45th Pennsylvania was one of many Union regiments to assail the Rebels in the tangled hell of the Wilderness. The 45th reached the enemy breastworks and planted its flag, but was forced to retreat. Captain Rees G. Richards was attempting to rally his company when he found Colonel John I. Curtin, distraught over the absence of the regimental flag. But soon, the color-bearer emerged through the acrid smoke, still carrying his bullet-ridden silk banner. Captain Richards, elated, seized the flag from the bearer and began to sing, "Rally round the flag, boys!/ Rally once again!/ Shouting the battle cry of freedom."

Other soldiers heard the captain and joined in. Soon, the entire regiment rallied as men hurried back into line, emboldened by the captain's singing. This incident, although seemingly trivial, shows how important a battle flag was to those who served beneath its folds. But these big infantry flags (in the Union army, 6 x 6½ feet in size) were ready-made targets for enemy fire. Color-bearers were slain by the score in large battles, and many Medals of Honor earned during the war were for actions involved in either saving or capturing flags.

Captain Rees G. Richards

Jackson's flank march took place on May 2, and even though Yankee skirmishers located the route of march and General Daniel Sickles sallied forth with the Third Corps to see what was going on, General Oliver O. Howard, commanding the Eleventh Corps on Hooker's right, failed to take any precautions against attack. Thus, when Jackson's troops charged forth shortly after 6:00 P.M., Howard's corps was routed and Sickles, hastily recalled, had to conduct a night battle to link up with the main line. That night, while reconnoitering in front of his troops, Jackson was badly wounded by his own men, who mistakenly thought they were being attacked by enemy horsemen.

General Thomas Jonathan "Stonewall" Jackson

May 3 saw desperate fighting around the Chancellor House as Hooker began to pull his army back into a tighter perimeter guarding the fords across the Rappahannock. The general himself was stunned when a shell struck a pillar on the Chancellor House porch, and even though subordinates wanted to counterattack the disorganized Confederates, Hooker was adamant about retreating. In the meantime, Union general John Sedgwick's Sixth Corps attacked at Fredericksburg, broke through the thinly manned defenses, and headed for Chancellorsville. Lee sent troops to oppose Sedgwick, and the two forces engaged in combat at Salem Church

BLOODY ANGLE'S OAK TREE

During the intense fighting at Spotsylvania on May 12, 1864, a sizeable oak tree between the lines eventually fell after being chipped away by bullet after bullet. The tree's demise was witnessed by hundreds of men who wrote about it in letters home or in postwar recollections. In May 1865, Union soldiers returning to Washington camped in the area and visited the site. Relic hunters quickly decimated the remains, and the oak stump had disappeared. General Nelson A. Miles traced it to a local innkeeper, who was persuaded to part with the souvenir. Miles presented the relic to Secretary of War Edwin M. Stanton. The stump is now in the collection of the Smithsonian Institution's National Museum of American History.

An ill-advised march through the mud by Union troops in January 1863 was one factor that led to the dismissal of General Ambrose Burnside from command of the Army of the Potomac.

The oak stump

before Sedgwick retreated and recrossed the Rappahannock on May 4.

Hooker's main army retreated to its old camps opposite Fredericksburg on May 6. His army lost 17,287 soldiers, while Lee's army counted 12,821 casualties. Stonewall Jackson's wounded arm was amputated and the general was healing well until pneumonia set in; he died in a small house near Guinea Station on May 10. General Lee said that he "lost [his] right arm" when Jackson died.

The area next saw fighting a year later, in May 1864. Lieutenant General Ulysses S. Grant, in charge of all the Union armies, directed General Meade's Army of the Potomac, supported by General Burnside's Ninth Corps, to cross the Rapidan from its camps near Brandy Station and move through the Wilderness toward Fredericksburg. Grant felt that the army could move rapidly and reach clear terrain before Lee could engage the troops in battle. Even if the Confederate troops reached them, Grant felt that his 115,000 men would be able to handle Lee's much smaller army.

Cavalry detected the Union advance and Lee moved from his camps south of the Rapidan to the east to confront the Yankees. Fighting erupted on May 5 as troops from the two armies collided on the Orange Turnpike. Here, two Union corps (the Fifth and Sixth) confronted Richard S. Ewell's corps from Lee's army. Farther south, General Winfield S. Hancock's Second Corps encountered troops from Ambrose P. Hill's Third Corps of Lee's army. By nightfall, battle lines were drawn and Lee awaited Longstreet's arrival from southwestern Virginia.

Fighting continued on May 5 as Hancock launched a massive attack that drove Hill back, but Longstreet's opportune arrival blunted the Yankees and forced a stalemate. Elsewhere, troops fighting in the tangled underbrush also had to contend with forest fires that threatened both sides and endangered the thousands of wounded men lying on the ground. The two days of fierce fighting cost Grant more than 18,000 men, with Lee's loss estimated at more than 8,000. However, instead of retreating, Grant ordered George Meade to move the army east, out of the Wilderness, heading around Lee's right flank.

General Winfield Hancock

Lee was forced to react and stay between Grant and the roads to Richmond. The two armies edged to the east and a series of battles took place between May 8 and 18, collectively called the Battle of Spotsylvania, named for the tiny village that served as the seat of Spotsylvania County. Confederate infantry from Longstreet's corps (now led by Richard H. Anderson after Longstreet's accidental wounding in the Wilderness) raced ahead to secure the crossroads, barely arriving before Union infantry began attacking on the afternoon of May 8 in an engagement sometimes called Laurel Hill. Lee's troops arrived and erected earthworks in the shape of a large inverted "U" as the Yankees took positions nearby.

Union attacks continued on May 10 but were mostly repulsed. At 6:00 P.M., Colonel Emory Upton led 12 regiments in a bayonet charge against the western face of the southern salient. Although Upton's charge broke into the enemy line, his outnumbered men were eventually forced back. But the attack gave Grant the idea to launch a much larger charge, this time using Hancock's entire Second Corps. This massive attack occurred as dawn broke on May 12. Rain soon set in, and although Hancock's initial charge shattered a Confederate division and seized several artillery batteries, it lost momentum as units became disorganized and southern troops rushed to fill the breach. The rest of the day saw one of the most savage conflicts of the war as troops engaged in bloody hand-to-hand combat, at times separated only by log breastworks. After dark, when the Rebels had constructed a new defensive line at the base of the salient, they fell back and the 20-hour-long battle sputtered to a close.

The two armies remained in position for another week. Grant ordered an attack on May 18, but many regiments went into the battle only halfheartedly before retreating from the formidable enemy earthworks. The general then decided to move the army to the east again, forcing Lee to abandon his strong position. On May 19, southern units probing the Union right flank encountered newly arrived regiments of heavy artillery from the Washington defenses. These artillerists had been given infantry equipment and sent to reinforce Grant. Although suffering severe casualties, these "heavies" slowed Ewell's attack long enough to enable reinforcements to arrive. Ewell then withdrew, and the fighting in the area was over as the armies headed south toward the North Anna River. Grant's army had lost more than 18,000 soldiers in the fighting at Spotsylvania, while Lee's casualties, although not reported as precisely, were at least 10,000. Grant was able to replace his losses, while Lee had difficulty finding reinforcements as his army dwindled in strength.

BATTLEFIELD PRESERVATION

The roots of Civil War battlefield preservation go back to 1864, when Pennsylvania chartered a private corporation to preserve portions of the Gettysburg battleground. Other private groups emerged, but in the 1890s the federal government acquired the Gettysburg, Antietam, Shiloh, Chickamauga, and Vicksburg battle sites. Other parks were created through the years and in 1933 were turned over to the National Park Service for administration. The 1960s centennial, a concurrent rise in tourism, and developmental expansion threats to many battlefields led to an increase in preservation activism. Arkansas political consultant Jerry Russell formed the Civil War Round Table Associates in the late 1960s to warn the public of commercial and residential threats to sacred ground. By the 1980s, other organizations had formed in response to the lack of federal money for preservation. In 1988 and 1994, threats to Manassas, Virginia, garnered national headlines as proponents of preservation turned aside commercial threats to this site's integrity. Some sites, such as Chantilly in Virginia and those around Atlanta, have been lost to urbanization, but an increased awareness of cultural heritage has led to other victories in the quest to preserve the battlefields of the 1860s.

VISITOR INFORMATION

Name Stones River

Classification National Battlefield

Established Park—March 3, 1927. Transferred from War Department August 10, 1933; redesignated April 22, 1960. Boundary changes: April 22, 1960; December 23, 1987; December 11, 1991.
Cemetery—Date of Civil War interments: 1865. Transferred from War Department August 10, 1933

Contact 3501 Old Nashville Highway, Murfreesboro, TN 37129

Phone 615-893-9501

Website www.nps.gov/stri

Acreage Park—708.32 (Federal: 494.10; Nonfederal: 214.13) Cemetery—20.09 (all Federal)

Points of Focus The Cotton Field, Defense of the Nashville Pike (Six-gun Chicago Board of Trade Battery), Fortress Rosecrans, Hazen Monument (Fight for the Round Forest), McFadden's Ford, The Slaughter Pen, Stones River National Cemetery

Tours/Paths Walking trails, self-guided driving tour

Hours Open daily from 8:00 A.M. to 5:00 P.M. Closed December 25

Park Fee Free

Programs Ranger-led walks and discussions (May to November), audiovisual orientation program

Facilities Visitor center, museum, recreation greenways

Major General William S. Rosecrans

STONES RIVER
CONTEST FOR MURFREESBORO

Following the unsuccessful Confederate invasion of Kentucky in October 1862 the Union Army of the Cumberland received a new commander, Major General William S. Rosecrans, an Ohio-born officer with previous successes in western Virginia and Mississippi. The new commander moved his army back to Nashville and divided it into three corps, led by generals George H. Thomas, Alexander M. McCook, and Thomas L. Crittenden.

Rosecrans's opponent was General Braxton Bragg and his Army of Tennessee, encamped near Murfreesboro, about 30 miles southeast of Nashville. Bragg's two corps commanders were generals Leonidas Polk and William J. Hardee. His 38,000 troops were outnumbered by Rosecrans's 44,000.

Goaded by the Lincoln administration to take some kind of action, Rosecrans finally began moving south on December 26, after beefing up his supply

The Hazen Brigade Monument, erected at Stones River in 1863, is the oldest intact Civil War monument still in its original location.

base at Nashville. By December 30, the Yankees had moved to within 2 miles of Murfreesboro, but a heavy rainstorm stalled their southward advance. Bragg concentrated his troops to oppose Rosecrans as the two armies drew near each other.

Instead of passively awaiting the Yankee attack, Bragg decided to launch a December 31 early-morning attack against the Union right flank. If all went according to plan, Hardee's troops would roll up the Union flank and drive the enemy back against the rain-swollen Stones River, which bisected Bragg's chosen battleground. But unbeknownst to Bragg, Rosecrans had decided on a similar maneuver. His left flank would strike Bragg's right and drive the Rebels away from Murfreesboro. The Yankee attack was likewise planned to start on December 31.

Bragg struck first. At dawn on the last day of 1862, Hardee's divisions charged and hit the Yankee right flank, shattering the first Federal units

The massed fire of 58 union guns like this smoothbore Napoleon cannon played a decisive role in repulsing the final Confederate attempt to recross Stones River after Union troops abandoned their defense of the Round Forest. The Confederates lost 1,700 of the 4,500 men who took part in the final attack.

MUTINY

In late summer 1862, Captain William J. Palmer began recruiting the 15th Pennsylvania Cavalry. Nicknamed the "Anderson Cavalry," Palmer's unit was intended to act as headquarters guard for General Robert Anderson, the hero of Fort Sumter. The unit began recruiting at Carlisle, Pennsylvania. Palmer was captured while scouting during the Antietam operations and the regiment was sent to Nashville. Although it lacked proper officers, the regiment was ordered to help the advance of Murfreesboro. But the men mutinied, saying they had enlisted only to act as headquarters guards. Still, majors Adolph Rosengarten and Frank Ward took 300 of the mutineers into action on December 29, heading the advance toward the enemy. The regiment encountered infantry and was repulsed; both majors were killed. The remaining 600 men were thrown in prison until General Rosecrans worked out a deal to get the regiment back to work. Palmer was exchanged in February 1863 and reorganized his regiment, but the mutiny attached a stigma to the 15th that was never completely erased.

General Robert Anderson

An idealized version of the Battle of Stones River in a Currier & Ives lithograph

they encountered. Richard Johnson's and Jefferson C. Davis's divisions were driven back toward Stones River by Hardee's troops. But Philip Sheridan's division of McCook's corps, although driven back, rallied and took position in the cedar woods around the Wilkinson Pike and held firm. Rosecrans hurried reinforcements into the widening battle and by afternoon, Rebel attacks slowed against mounting numbers of Yankees and on account of their own disorganization. Soldiers dubbed one section of an area along the tracks of the Nashville & Chattanooga Railroad line "Hell's Half Acre" because of the intense close combat

there. By evening, the southerners had withdrawn and reformed.

Bragg expected that Rosecrans would withdraw because his army was in a precarious position, with its back to Stones River. But the Union general merely straightened his line and remained on the field, daring Bragg to resume the contest. Rosecrans even established a new position on the opposite side of the river that would enable his artillery to enfilade any attacking columns.

Angered by his enemy's unwillingness to retreat, Bragg sent Brigadier General John C. Breckinridge's division across the river to capture the new enemy

> ## "Men fell around on every side like autumn leaves and every foot of soil over which we passed seemed dyed with the life blood of some one or more of the gallant spirits whom I had the honor to command."
>
> *—Lieutenant Colonel J. J. Scales, 30th Mississippi*

line. Breckinridge protested but launched his brigades into action late on the afternoon of January 2, 1863. Although suffering some loss, his troops drove the enemy from a low ridge and toward the river. But Major John Mendenhall, a Union artillery commander, had deployed 57 cannons across the stream in anticipation of such an emergency. His gunners blasted Breckinridge's troops as Yankee reinforcements splashed across the stream to recapture the ridge. After losing 1,700 men in less than an hour, Breckinridge, lacking reinforcements, fell back to his initial position.

The two armies again spent a cold, restless night sleeping on their weapons in anticipation of more action. On January 3, heeding the advice of his generals, Bragg decided to withdraw. His army had lost a total of 9,870 officers and men killed, wounded, and captured, a casualty rate of 26 percent. Rosecrans's casualty list totaled some 12,706 officers

and men, 29 percent of his effective strength on the battlefield. Both sides claimed victory, but by withdrawing, Bragg conceded the field to Rosecrans, who did not pursue because of his own casualties and a postbattle heavy rain. The Union victory at Stones River provided welcome news to Northerners who had read of defeats at Fredericksburg, Virginia, and Grant's initial failure in his operations at Vicksburg, Mississippi.

Kurz & Allison print of the Battle of Stones River

CHAPLAIN JOHN M. WHITEHEAD

During the Civil War, fifteen Union army chaplains were killed or mortally wounded and four received Congressional Medals of Honor. One of these four was Chaplain John M. Whitehead of the 15th Indiana. During the fighting at Stones' River, Whitehead, a Baptist minister, displayed great bravery in helping carry wounded men from the battle line as well as comforting dying men of his unit, which suffered heavy casualties. Captain Joel Foster, a peacetime neighbor from Westville, Indiana, fell mortally wounded into Whitehead's arms during the intense fighting in "Hell's Half Acre." Lieutenant Colonel Isaac Suman of the 9th Indiana was shot twice; Whitehead found the badly wounded officer and managed to extract a lead bullet from his side, then stanched the flow of blood from both wounds. "When Chaplain Whitehead gave me his assistance," recalled Suman, "he was all besmeared with the blood of the wounded he had cared for. He seemed to be an angel among the wounded, Yankees and Johnnies alike."

Chaplain John M. Whitehead

A part of the Wisconsin State memorial at Vicksburg, shown here on a hazy, gray day. The memorial commemorates the sacrifices of over 9,000 soldiers from that state who fought here in 1862–63.

VICKSBURG

UNVEXED TO THE SEA

VISITOR INFORMATION

Name Vicksburg

Classification National Military Park

Established Park—February 21, 1899. Transferred from War Department August 10, 1933. Boundary changes: June 4, 1963; October 18, 1990. Cemetery—Date of Civil War interments: 1866–74. Transferred from War Department August 10, 1933. Boundary change: March 2, 1955

Contact 3201 Clay Street, Vicksburg, MS 39188

Phone 601-636-0583

Website www.nps.gov/vick

Acreage Park—1,736.47 (Federal: 1,729.63; Nonfederal: 6.84) Cemetery—11.63 (all Federal)

Points of Focus Battery Selfridge, Battery De Golyer, Fort Hill, Fort Garrott, Great Redoubt, Hovey's Approach, Railroad Redoubt, Ransom's Gun Path, Second Texas Lunette, Shirley House, Stockade Redan Attack, Stockade Redan, Thayer's Approach, Third Louisiana Redan, Vicksburg National Cemetery, USS *Cairo*

Tours/Paths 16-mile self-guided driving tour

Hours Open daily from 8:00 A.M. to 5:00 P.M. Closed December 25

Park Fee $3 per person or $5 per vehicle

Programs USS *Cairo* film at USS *Cairo* Museum, audiovisual orientation film at visitor center, Living History program (summer season only)

Facilities Visitor center, USS *Cairo* Museum, picnic areas, bookstore

Considered by many historians to be the turning point of the Civil War, the campaign for Vicksburg, Mississippi, lasted from November 1862 until its surrender on July 4, 1863. General Ulysses S. Grant, in command of the Union Army of the Tennessee, was pitted against General John C. Pemberton, the Confederate general tasked with protecting Mississippi from invasion.

Vicksburg was situated on a high bluff overlooking a sharp bend in the Mississippi River. Its fortifications, which included several cannon batteries, controlled ship traffic on the river below. Seizing Vicksburg would go a long way in severing the Trans-Mississippi states from the rest of the Confederacy, as well as providing a water route for commodities to reach foreign markets from the Midwest.

The siege of Vicksburg

Grant began his campaign from northern Mississippi in November 1862, intending to march overland to attack the city from the rear. But Confederate cavalry led by Earl Van Dorn raided Grant's supply base at Holly Springs, forcing Grant to retreat. General William T. Sherman, in command of one of Grant's wings, had gone down the Mississippi by boat and landed his troops just above the city, but his December 29 attack at Chickasaw Bluffs was repelled. Grant then marched to join Sherman at the new base of Milliken's Bend, upriver and on the opposite side from Vicksburg.

Grant had about 35,000 men available for duty after leaving behind enough troops to protect Memphis and other points in the rear. Throughout the winter of 1862–63, Grant sent expeditions into the bayous west of the Mississippi in a vain effort to find an alternative route around Vicksburg's

THE CIVIL WAR

THE USS *CAIRO*

This river ironclad, one of seven nicknamed "Pook's Turtles" after their designer, were in essence armored rafts with a shallow draft that enabled them to operate on the Mississippi River and its tributaries. The *Cairo* was 175 feet long, powered by a stern paddlewheel, and mounted 13 cannons. The ship's heavy armor limited her to a mere 5 knots. She was engaged in battle at Fort Pillow and Memphis, Tennessee, before steaming south to assist in the reduction of Vicksburg. In December 1862, the *Cairo* became the first warship to be sunk by an electrically detonated torpedo when she steamed over two enemy torpedoes positioned in the Yazoo River north of Vicksburg. The ship sank upright in 36 feet of water with no casualties. Rediscovered, the *Cairo* was raised in 1965 and after extensive conservation, was placed on display in the Vicksburg National Military Park in 1977.

defenses. One such attempt included digging a canal across the base of the peninsula opposite Vicksburg and diverting the river channel, but high water flooded the canal before it was finished.

After these efforts failed, Grant decided to move his army downriver and try to cross below Vicksburg. Sherman's corps remained behind as a diversion while Grant's other two corps, led by generals James B. McPherson and John A. McClernand, began the strenuous task of filtering through the bayous. To further distract Pemberton, Grant sent Colonel Benjamin H. Grierson's cavalry on a raid through central Mississippi, wrecking telegraph lines, tearing up railroads, and forcing Pemberton's cavalry to chase him. Grierson's cavalry eventually reached Union lines at Baton Rouge after accomplishing their task.

On April 16, 1863, Union admiral David D. Porter's fleet steamed past the Vicksburg batteries, suffering minor damage. Porter's gunboats protected several troop transports sent to ferry Grant's troops across the river. Two weeks later a local contraband slave told Grant about a crossing place at Bruinsburg. Grant crossed there as Sherman's men marched to join the other two corps. On May 1, McClernand

and McPherson attacked Confederate troops led by General John S. Bowen, whose men blocked roads leading to Port Gibson. After a sharp engagement, Bowen was forced to retreat to Grand Gulf.

Grant then decided to march inland rather than doing the expected—move north directly upon Vicksburg. The general felt that he needed to disperse any southern troops nearby and to try to isolate Pemberton's large garrison. Accordingly, Grant's army headed northeast. McPherson's corps encountered a lone Rebel brigade, commanded by John Gregg, at the village of Raymond on May 12. McPherson's men drove Gregg away and continued on toward Jackson, the state capital. Here, General Joseph E. Johnston had begun to gather troops to support Pemberton. But Johnston had only about 6,000 men, and when Grant attacked on May 14, Johnston delayed long enough to evacuate the city and retreat to the north. The Yankees occupied Jackson briefly, wrecking railroads and burning industries before heading west toward Vicksburg.

McPherson and McClernand encountered Pemberton with 22,000 men at Champion's Hill. This May 16 battle was the largest of the campaign. Superior Union numbers pushed the enemy off the field. Pemberton suffered 3,624 casualties, and one of his divisions was largely cut off during the retreat and marched to join Johnston. Grant struck again on the seventeenth at the Big Black River, launching a devastating attack that inflicted 1,024 casualties—mostly captured—on Pemberton's rearguard.

Pemberton withdrew into Vicksburg's formidable defenses. Grant, believing that his adversary was demoralized, attacked on May 19. However, his assaults were repelled with a loss of 942 men. Undeterred, Grant authorized another attack on May 22. He wanted to avoid a siege because of the menace of Johnston's growing army at his rear.

The USS Cairo

Accordingly, his men assaulted on a front of 3 miles. Heavy fighting surged around Confederate earthworks such as the Stockade Redan, the Great Redoubt, and the Railroad Redoubt. At this last place, Yankee soldiers swarmed in and drove off its defenders, but Texas troops counterattacked, and after a melee involving clubbed muskets, hand grenades, and bayonets, drove out the bluecoats. Union losses totaled 3,199.

Grant then extended his line and put the city and its garrison under siege. By the end of June, Grant's army had grown to 75,000 men. Porter's gunboats kept the city under fire and provided crews to man some of the Union siege batteries. Union troops began digging zigzag approach trenches to get closer to the southern lines, but sharpshooters and the use of hand grenades made the going slow. Union soldiers also dug tunnels and exploded mines under two Confederate forts, but neither explosion helped rupture the enemy lines.

By late June, the state of affairs within Vicksburg was growing desperate. Food was rapidly disappearing, the city newspaper resorted to using wallpaper to print its last issues, and many citizens dug caves in order to escape the incessant shelling that was reducing the city to rubble. Pemberton wanted to break out of the city and join Johnston, but with more than 10,000 men on the sick lists, and a shortage of rations, it meant his forces were too weak for active operations.

The Union assault on May 22, 1863

So, on July 3, Pemberton raised a flag of truce and sought an audience with Grant. After some brief negotiating, Pemberton decided to surrender his 29,000 men on the condition that they would be paroled and sent home to await proper exchange as prisoners of war. The formal surrender took place on July 4. Grant then sent Sherman east against Johnston, who again evacuated Jackson after holding off the Yankees for a few days. When Port Hudson, Louisiana, surrendered to troops under General Nathaniel P. Banks on July 9, the entire stretch of the Mississippi was again under Union control.

Grant, who undertook many risks and emerged victorious, brilliantly executed the Vicksburg campaign. As a result, he was promoted to the command of all Union troops west of the Appalachians, the first step in his rise to general-in-chief by March 1864.

JOHN C. PEMBERTON

Despite his lack of battlefield experience, John C. Pemberton was promoted to lieutenant general and sent to defend Vicksburg in 1862. There he had initial success in the field, fending off Union forces until spring 1863, when two bloody defeats drove him back into the city to endure the 47-day siege. Pemberton, called a traitor in the South for surrendering Vicksburg (the general was originally from Philadelphia but had married a Virginia woman), asked for a court of inquiry but never received a hearing. He resigned his general's commission and was reappointed a lieutenant colonel of artillery in the spring of 1864, serving initially in the defenses of Richmond.

After the war, Pemberton farmed in Virginia before returning to Philadelphia. His citizenship was restored in 1879. Pemberton died in 1881 and is buried in Philadelphia's Laurel Hill Cemetery. He wrote a memoir that defended his actions during the war, but it was only recently discovered and was not published until 1999.

John C. Pemberton

VISITOR INFORMATION

Name Gettysburg

Classification National Military Park

Established Park—February 11, 1895. Transferred from War Department August 10, 1933. Boundary changes: January 31, 1948; July 31, 1953; April 1, 1974. Cemetery—Date of Civil War interments: 1863. Transferred from War Department August 10, 1933. Boundary changes: June 19, 1948; August 17, 1990

Contact 97 Taneytown Road, Gettysburg, PA 17325

Phone 717-334-1124

Website www.nps.gov/gett

Acreage Park—5,989.09 (Federal: 4,179.33; Nonfederal: 1,809.76). Cemetery—20.58 (all Federal)

Points of Focus Barlow Knoll, East Cavalry Battlefield Site, East Cemetery Hill, Eternal Light Peace Memorial, High Water Mark Trail, Johnny Reb Trail, Little Round Top, McPherson's Ridge, National Cemetery, North Carolina Memorial, Oak Ridge, Pitzer Woods, Spangler's Spring, Virginia Memorial, Warfield Ridge, Yank Trail

Tours/Paths Self-guided driving tour; Licensed Battlefield Guide tour (fee); various hiking, biking, and horse trails

Hours Open daily from 8:00 A.M. to 5:00 P.M. Closed Thanksgiving Day, December 25, and January 1

Park Fee Free

Programs 20-minute Cyclorama Center presentation ($3 fee), two free battle films in the Cyclorama Center, 30-minute Electronic Map orientation program ($4 fee), Junior Ranger program

Facilities Cyclorama Center, amphitheater, campsite, two picnic areas, visitor center, bookstore, museum

GETTYSBURG

A NEW BIRTH OF FREEDOM

Following the Battle of Chancellorsville in May 1863, General Robert E. Lee reorganized his army into three corps, led by lieutenant generals James Longstreet, Richard S. Ewell, and Ambrose P. Hill. Strengthened by new brigades, his Army of Northern Virginia fielded about 75,000 men, the strongest it had been in over a year.

Union general Joseph Hooker's Army of the Potomac remained a threat. Although defeated in the recent battle, Hooker's army maintained high morale and troops that were anxious to engage in combat again. But the army began to shrink as nine-month and two-year regiments mustered out, taking about 20,000 soldiers from the ranks.

Lee had planned to march into Maryland again, but Hooker's movement preempted his plans. The Confederate general sought to draw the armies away from war-ravaged northern Virginia, gather supplies north of the Mason-Dixon Line, and perhaps win a victory on Northern soil. Since Europeans withheld recognition at this stage of the war, Lee reasoned that a southern victory might convince the Lincoln administration to sue for peace.

The campaign in Gettysburg began in early June, as Lee began to shift troops away from Fredericksburg toward the Shenandoah Valley. Hooker sent his cavalry across the Rappahannock on June 9, engaging Jeb Stuart's southern horsemen in a day-long battle at Brandy Station. Ewell's corps struck the Federal garrison at Winchester, shattering the Yankees and sending survivors running. Ewell's three divisions continued across the Potomac and into southern Pennsylvania. Meanwhile, Hooker's army headed north as cavalry from the opposing sides fought at Aldie, Middleburg, and Upperville.

As the rest of Lee's army moved across the Potomac, Hooker followed more slowly, unsure of Lee's intentions. The general had orders to protect Washington, but Hooker also wanted to use the Harper's Ferry garrison and part of his army to sever Lee's supply line with Virginia. When the War Department refused Hooker's request, he sent in his resignation. Lincoln accepted Hooker's tender and replaced

General George G. Meade

The 40th New York infantry "Mozarters" are memorialized at Gettysburg. The unit fought in the battle and took part in Meade's cautious pursuit of Lee afterward. They were called "Mozarters" after the political faction in New York—Mozart, a rival group to Tammany Hall—which funded the outfitting, training, and transportation of the men.

BATTLEFIELD MONUMENTS

At present, there are 1,328 monuments, markers, and tablets on the Gettysburg battlefield. The first monument, in the shape of a memorial urn, was placed in the National Cemetery by survivors of the 1st Minnesota regiment in 1869. A decade later, the 2nd Massachusetts erected the first monument on the battlefield proper when the survivors placed it to mark the regiment's position on July 3 near Spangler's Spring. Most memorials were erected during the 1880s and 1890s. The latest additions, a monument and a position marker, were erected by descendants of the 11th Mississippi and were placed on the field in 2000. In 2002, a bronze sculpture by Ron Tunison was unveiled in the town's Evergreen Cemetery, honoring women of Gettysburg. It depicts Elizabeth Thorn, the cemetery caretaker's wife, mopping her brow, a shovel in her hand. Her husband was in the Union army. Thorn, six months pregnant, aided by her aged father, buried 91 bodies in the town cemetery.

North Carolina State Monument

him with Major General George G. Meade on June 28, as the army gathered near Frederick, Maryland.

Lee's army, by late June, was mostly in the vicinity of Chambersburg, Pennsylvania, while Ewell's corps was scattered, a division at York and two divisions approaching the western defenses of Harrisburg, which was defended by state militia called into service in response to Lee's invasion. Troops from New York also flocked into the area to oppose a Confederate advance. But very quickly one of Longstreet's spies managed bring word that the enemy was across the Potomac and heading north under a new general. Lee recalled Ewell's units and began to concentrate his army just to the east of Chambersburg.

Upon taking command, Meade brought his army closer together and contemplated fighting a defensive battle behind the line of Pipe Creek, Maryland. But he gave his subordinates discretionary orders as well. On June 30, Union cavalry led by John Buford entered the crossroads town of Gettysburg and sighted enemy troops to the

John B. Bachelder created this isometric view of Gettysburg in the fall of 1863.

west on the Chambersburg Pike. The next morning, July 1, Confederate troops from Hill's corps appeared on the road to Gettysburg and engaged Buford's cavalry, fighting dismounted. Buford's outnumbered troopers held off the first Confederate attacks until infantry from Major General John F. Reynolds's First Corps arrived on the scene and counterattacked, shattering two Confederate brigades and capturing one of their

THE COLORFUL LIFE OF DAN SICKLES

Daniel E. Sickles (1819–1914) was a Democratic politician who was given a general's commission by the Lincoln administration to help bolster support for the war effort. Sickles was already well-known when the war began. As secretary to the American delegation in London, he took a New York prostitute with him and actually presented her to Queen Victoria. In 1859, Sickles shot and killed Philip Barton Key (Francis Scott Key's son), who had been having an affair with his wife. In the ensuing trial, his lawyers pleaded temporary insanity for the first time in American legal history and their client was acquitted. Sickles was wounded at Gettysburg, losing his right leg to a cannonball. He later gave the amputated limb to the Army Medical Museum, where it now reposes.

After the war, Sickles was American minister to Spain and helped establish a short-lived Spanish republic, but rumors of an affair with Queen Isabella II compromised his effectiveness. In later years, Sickles was again serving in Congress and authored the bill that established the Gettysburg National Military Park. But as chairman of the New York Gettysburg Battlefield Commission, he was accused of embezzlement and removed. Sickles's efforts to smear General Meade's name and accomplishments at Gettysburg have typified Sickles's extremely controversial life.

commanders. Reynolds was killed early in the action and was replaced by his senior division commander, Abner Doubleday. The Union Eleventh Corps arrived and extended the First Corps line north of Gettysburg.

After a lull in the fighting, more Confederates arrived, another division of Hill's corps and two of Ewell's, all returning from their abortive march on Harrisburg. Ewell's troops struck the Eleventh Corps line, outflanked it, and routed some of its

units, pursuing the fugitives through the streets of Gettysburg. Meanwhile, the outnumbered First Corps inflicted and received heavy casualties as Hill's divisions pushed it, too, back through Gettysburg. The survivors were beginning to regroup on Cemetery Hill south of the town when Winfield Scott Hancock, Meade's Second Corps commander, arrived on the field, sent there by Meade to assess the situation. Hancock helped get the troops in order as units from two more Federal

SERGEANT AMOS HUMISTON

Amos Humiston was a member of Company C, 154th New York, a regiment that served in the ill-fated Eleventh Corps at Gettysburg. Humiston's regiment and the rest of its brigade rushed into the town to cover the retreat of the broken corps on the afternoon of July 1. The brigade was drawn up in battle line when it was overwhelmed by attacking Confederates. Sergeant Humiston's body was found in Stratton Street after Union soldiers reoccupied the town. Clutched in his hand was a photograph of his three children, the last thing the sergeant saw before he died. But no personal information was found on Humiston's body. Who were the children? The body was buried and the photograph was copied and circulated widely throughout the North. Finally, Humiston's widow, living in Cattaraugus County, New York, saw the photo and identified the children as her own. Proceeds from the sale of this now-famous photo were used to found the Soldiers Orphans Home at Gettysburg. The widow Humiston was its first matron.

The Humiston children

A scene from the Gettysburg cyclorama, showing Union troops advancing

corps arrived. He recommended fighting at Gettysburg, a decision Meade had already made, having sent orders to the rest of the army to march there.

Throughout the night, units of the two armies converged on Gettysburg. By early morning of July 2, Meade had fashioned a J-shaped line of battle, stretching from Culp's Hill on the right to nearby Cemetery Hill to the west, then southward along Cemetery Ridge to Little Round Top, a jagged hill partially cleared of timber by local farmers. Meade planned to wait until his entire army was on the field before attacking—his biggest corps, John Sedgwick's Sixth, was more than 30 miles away and would not reach the field until later that day.

Lee, forced into an unwanted battle by his subordinates, nevertheless concentrated his army and decided to attack the enemy against the wishes of Longstreet, his most trusted corps commander. Lee felt he could not afford to wait for Meade's attack because of a lack of supplies and his fear that enemy militia might move upon his rear flank. Besides, Lee thought his veteran soldiers could whip the Yankees in a fair fight. Lee ordered Longstreet to take his two divisions (George Pickett's was still en route) and attack up the Emmitsburg Road toward Cemetery Hill. Faulty reconnaissance led Lee to believe that Meade's line did not extend all the way south along Cemetery Ridge. Thus, Longstreet would assail Meade's left while Ewell attacked Culp's Hill to pin the enemy in place. Hill's corps, in the center, would assist the other two corps and attack if the opportunity presented itself.

Subsequent maneuvers on both sides remain enshrouded in controversy. Longstreet waited for direct orders and did not begin his march until 11:00 A.M. By the time his lead brigade arrived in the vicinity of the Emmitsburg Road (after taking a circuitous route to avoid being seen by Federal signal corpsmen on Little Round Top), Longstreet found that the enemy had moved forward to occupy high ground along that road. Union major general Daniel E. Sickles, a politically minded general with no prior military training, was in charge of Meade's Third Corps. Sickles was assigned to that part of the line south of Hancock on Cemetery Ridge, but he did not like his position and after much wrangling with Meade and other officers, took it upon himself to move forward to seize high ground along the Emmitsburg Road, thereby ignoring Little Round Top and placing his command forward of the main Union line. His corps were arrayed in a V-shaped salient.

Meade did not learn of Sickles's mid-afternoon move until later, when he convened a meeting of his corps commanders and discovered that Sickles had moved forward. Sickles offered to return to the main line, but at 3:30 P.M., Longstreet's artillery opened fire. Meade told Sickles to remain in line and went back to bring up reinforcements. By the time the fighting died down after nightfall, Meade had sent in five brigades from Hancock's Second Corps, the entire Fifth Corps, some of the depleted First Corps, a division from the Twelfth Corps, and brigades from the tired Sixth Corps as they arrived on the field. Longstreet's eight brigades,

General James Longstreet

assisted by one of Hill's divisions, fought all these Union troops. Union troops reached Little Round Top just minutes before Confederate troops attacked, saving the Union left flank. Combat swirled back and forth across a 19-acre wheatfield (later called "The Wheatfield"), among the boulders of Devil's Den, and in farmer Sherfy's Peach Orchard. Sickles himself was hit in the leg by a cannonball; his shattered limb was later amputated. By day's end, the Union line had stabilized on Cemetery Ridge.

On the Union right, Edward Johnson's division charged forward to occupy abandoned Union breastworks of the Twelfth Corps on Culp's Hill, but a lone New York brigade held the crest of the hill. Reinforcements and darkness neutralized further Confederate gains. Other southern regiments charged the Union batteries on Cemetery Hill, but were repelled after a vicious hand-to-hand fight.

THE GETTYSBURG GUN

During the terrific artillery duel preceding Pickett's Charge on the afternoon of July 3, an exploding ball from a Confederate cannon struck the muzzle of one of the 12-pounder Napoleon cannons in Battery B, 1st Rhode Island, killing two of its crewmen. The survivors removed their comrades and prepared to fire another round. But as they loaded their own solid shot into the muzzle, it became stuck because the enemy round had dented the barrel. The cannon was retired and retained as a trophy, and is on display today in the Rhode Island State House. Only a few years ago, the cannon was subjected to an X-ray scan. It was discovered that the barrel contained two powder charges that dated back to that fateful July day in 1863.

The Gettysburg Gun on display in the Rhode Island State House

AN ASSASSIN AT GETTYSBURG

Nineteen-year-old Lewis Powell (alias Lewis Paine) marched into battle on July 2 with the 3nd Florida infantry, part of Colonel David Lang's brigade of Richard Anderson's division. Lang's three regiments encountered a Union artillery battery supported by the 19th Maine regiment. Before the Yankees fell back to Cemetery Ridge, they inflicted numerous casualties on the Floridians. Private Powell was hit in the right wrist by a rifle ball and was captured when Lee's army retreated. Powell eventually was moved into a Baltimore hospital. After recovering sufficiently, he worked as a hospital assistant and befriended a nurse, who possibly helped him escape from watching guards. On April 14, 1865, as John Wilkes Booth assassinated President Lincoln, Powell barged into the home of Secretary of State William H. Seward and attacked him. The wounded Seward survived, but Powell was caught and hanged along with three others convicted in the assassination plot.

That night, Meade and his corps commanders decided to stay and fight one more day. Lee, believing that Meade had weakened his center to stabilize his flanks, ordered Longstreet to assail the Federal center.

Fighting on July 3 erupted at daybreak when Union troops attacked the Confederates on Culp's Hill. By late morning, the firing had died down as the Confederates withdrew, their attacks having been repulsed by the Yankees. Meanwhile Confederate artillerist Edward Porter Alexander assembled a line of 120 cannons to bombard the Union center. The Rebel guns opened fire shortly after one o'clock; more than 80 Union cannons replied. The thunderous bombardment shook the ground and reportedly could be heard as far away as Pittsburgh and Philadelphia. The resulting thick smoke obscured targets and misled southern cannoneers, who generally overshot Cemetery Ridge, thus causing havoc behind the Union lines.

As the bombardment died out, Longstreet sent George Pickett's three Virginia brigades forward, supported by troops from two of Hill's divisions. These units, estimated at between 10,500 and

General James E. B. Stuart

15,000 men, marched bravely across the mile-wide valley between Seminary and Cemetery ridges, being blasted the entire way by Union artillery. As the survivors crossed the Emmitsburg Road, Union musketry took its toll. By the time the advance elements reached the Union line, Pickett's Charge had been disrupted. Union counterattacks flanked both ends of the southern line, and the attack collapsed after briefly penetrating the Union line near a copse of trees. Half the attackers had been killed, wounded, or captured.

Pickett's Charge became the decisive repulsion of Lee's army. East of Gettysburg Jeb Stuart's horsemen moved to attack the Union rear but were countered by Yankee mounted troops led by David Gregg and George A. Custer. After a spirited battle, Stuart withdrew. A belated Union cavalry attack on the Confederate right failed, bringing to an end the three days of Gettysburg.

Meade's army of approximately 85,000 men suffered a loss of 22,807 (3,149 killed, 14,501 wounded, 5,157 captured or missing). Lee, with a battlefield strength of around 75,000, lost at least 28,000 soldiers. His army remained in position on

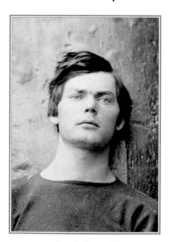

Lewis Powell

The rock pile called the Devil's Den, where hidden Confederate snipers harassed Union troops on Little Round Top

President Lincoln, who accepted the invitation to say a few words.

After listening to Everett for two hours, Lincoln arose to deliver his own speech. The president's now-famous Gettysburg Address contained just 272 words and lasted about two minutes. Its brevity meant photographers were unable to capture Lincoln's speech, but Everett quickly realized that the president, in his own folksy style, had articulated to his nation the higher ideals for which the war was being waged. Everett recognized that history would remember that speech longer than his own. "All men are created equal," said the president. This civil war was being fought to preserve the nation and its experiment in republican government. The war would produce a "new birth of freedom." Thus, "government of the people, by the people, for the people, shall not perish from the earth."

Lee's retreat as sketched by Albert Bobbett in 1905

July 4, but that night, in the midst of a hard rain, it began a retreat to Virginia. Meade, his army badly battered, followed but was unable to bring Lee to battle. Rain swelled the Potomac River and Union cavalry cut Lee's pontoon bridge, but the Confederates dug in and gave Meade's army cause for caution. By the time Meade was ready to attack, Lee had slipped across the Potomac. By the end of July, both armies were back in northern Virginia. The Gettysburg Campaign, though a bitter defeat for Lee, did not end the war.

Northerners quickly realized the significance of the battle and began to plan for a park to preserve the battlefield. Union dead were gathered together in a new cemetery adjacent to the civilian Evergreen Cemetery on Cemetery Hill. Formal dedication ceremonies were planned for the afternoon of November 19. The featured speaker was noted orator Edward Everett. Almost as an afterthought, somebody thought to invite

THE MASCOT OF THE 1ST MARYLAND

Union general Thomas L. Kane recorded the following incident as Rebels charged his brigade on Culp's Hill during the fierce fighting on the morning of July 3: "A pet dog belonging to a company of the 1st Maryland (Confederate) charged with the regiment, ran ahead of them when their progress was arrested, and came in among the boys in blue, as if the dog supposed they were what in better days they might have been—merely men of another noisy hose or engine company, competing for precedence with his masters in the smoke of a burning building. At first, some of my men said, he barked in valorous glee; but I myself first saw him on three legs going between our own and the men in gray on the ground as though looking for a dead master, or seeking on which side he might find an explanation of the tragedy he had witnessed, intelligible to his canine apprehension. Regarding him as the only Christian-minded being on either side, I ordered him to be honorably buried."

The Battle of Culp's Hill at Gettysburg

This Kurz & Allison print of the Battle of Chickamauga depicts the fierce confrontation as Confederate troops break through the Union lines on September 20, 1863.

CHICKAMAUGA

CONFEDERATE HIGH TIDE

VISITOR INFORMATION

Name Chickamauga & Chattanooga

Classification National Military Park

Established August 19, 1890. Transferred from War Department August 10, 1933. Boundary changes: August 9, 1939; March 5, 1942; June 24, 1948

Contact P.O. Box 2128, Fort Oglethorpe, GA 30742

Phone 706-866-9241

Website www.nps.gov/chch

Acreage 8,119.11 (Federal: 8,102.32; Nonfederal: 16.79)

Points of Focus Brotherton Cabin, Chattanooga National Cemetery, Cravens House, Lookout Mountain, Missionary Ridge, Orchard Knob, Snodgrass Hill, Sunset Rock, Wilder Brigade Monument

Tours/Paths 7-mile self-guided driving tour, various hiking and horse trails

Hours Open daily from 8:00 A.M. to 4:45 P.M. Closed December 25

Park Fee Free ($3 admission charge for Point Park)

Programs Living History programs, 26-minute orientation film, Junior Ranger program

Facilities Point Park, two visitor centers

Following the Battle of Stones River, Major General William S. Rosecrans's Union Army of the Cumberland went into winter quarters at Murfreesboro and rebuilt its strength. General Braxton Bragg's Army of Tennessee retreated from the area and went into position in the interior of Tennessee, some 40 miles from Murfreesboro. Here the armies stayed even as President Lincoln badgered Rosecrans to resume the offensive to ensure that Rebel reinforcements did not advance to Vicksburg or join Lee's Virginia army.

Rosecrans finally began to move in June 1863. In a series of brilliant maneuvers known as the Tullahoma Campaign, the Yankee general pushed Bragg's army out of central Tennessee with a minimum of fighting. Bragg retreated to Chattanooga and prepared to face Rosecrans. But Rosecrans failed to pursue Bragg and instead sent his three corps through the mountains west and southwest

Umbrella Rock on Lookout Mountain

of the city, threatening Bragg's supplies. Bragg hurriedly evacuated Chattanooga and withdrew into northern Georgia.

Rosecrans's mobile field army of some 58,000 men began to withdraw slightly once the general realized that his three corps were spaced too far apart to support one another. Bragg was being reinforced from Mississippi, Alabama, and Virginia; General Lee dispatched General James Longstreet and two divisions by rail to help him. When these troops arrived, Bragg's army actually outnumbered the Federals, a rarity in Civil War battles.

Rosecrans collected his troops on the west side of Chickamauga Creek, some 20 miles south of Chattanooga. Bragg planned to cross the creek north of Rosecrans's left flank and sever Union communications with Chattanooga. This would force Rosecrans to retreat westward through the mountains, thus allowing Bragg's troops to isolate and destroy the Yankees.

General Braxton Bragg

A MEDAL OF HONOR

First Lieutenant Arthur MacArthur of the 24th Wisconsin was only 18 years old when his regiment charged up the steep slopes of Missionary Ridge. When the color bearer fell down' exhausted, MacArthur grabbed the silk banner and led his men forward, shouting "On, Wisconsin!" as Confederate cannons blasted the attackers with canister. MacArthur planted the regimental flag on the enemy breastworks as his regiment swept over the crest of the ridge. In 1890, he received a Medal of Honor for his heroic deeds that day. MacArthur was later promoted to colonel of the regiment. His son, Douglas, was the famous army commander in the Pacific during World War II and in Korea.

First Lieutenant Arthur MacArthur Jr.

But Bragg's plan went awry from the beginning, and the anticipated battle did not materialize until September 19. On that day, Bragg's right wing under command of Lieutenant General Leonidas Polk, crossed the creek and assailed the Federal left flank, the first attack in a series of charges and countercharges that took place all along the 4-mile lines of battle. Rosecrans had stationed Major General George H. Thomas and his Fourteenth Corps on the Union left. Thomas, one of the Union's all-around best corps commanders, deployed his men in the densely wooded terrain and repelled all of Polk's attacks. Farther south more southern troops went into action, but by the end of the day all attacks had been repulsed. But Longstreet's troops began to arrive that night, giving Bragg the resolve to renew combat.

Fighting resumed on September 20, as Polk's troops hurled themselves against Thomas's line once more. Thomas began to call upon Rosecrans for reinforcements for his hard-pressed men. One of Rosecrans's staff officers then mistakenly told the general that there was a gap in the Union line farther south; in fact the officer had simply missed seeing the line, which had been hidden by dense trees. Rosecrans then ordered General Thomas J. Wood to take his division out of line and fill in the gap. Wood was dumbfounded—there were troops on his left. But the order was imperative, and he had earlier been castigated for not obeying orders with alacrity. Rather than argue with his superior, Wood complied.

As Wood's troops vacated the line and moved north, Longstreet's troops rolled forward and struck the gap Wood had created. The southern

Major General George H. Thomas

attack overwhelmed the Union right flank, which cracked under the pressure, and regiments retreated from the field toward Chattanooga, including Rosecrans and two of his corps commanders. Jubilant Confederates captured dozens of cannons as the army in blue melted away.

But Thomas's corps continued to hold its ground, strengthened by individual units that rallied and extended his line to cover the vital Snodgrass Hill. General Gordon Granger, acting without orders, brought fresh reserve brigades onto the field and went into position with Thomas. The entire Confederate army then assailed Thomas, but the Union line held until dark, when Thomas retired to Chattanooga. The general fairly earned his sobriquet "The Rock of Chickamauga."

Union casualties totaled 16,179, but Bragg's victorious army suffered a loss of 17,804 soldiers. Bragg followed Rosecrans to Chattanooga, a city he put under siege by occupying the high ground of Missionary Ridge and Lookout Mountain, which dominated the city and restricted access to the besieged defenders.

Rosecrans was relieved of command and replaced by Thomas. General Grant, having been placed in command of all Union forces west of the Appalachians following his victory at Vicksburg, arrived on the scene in person to direct operations.

Behind Grant came General William T. Sherman with more than 15,000 troops from Grant's army in Mississippi. From Virginia, Major General Joseph Hooker was placed in command of units from two corps from Meade's army that were sent by rail from northern Virginia to Bridgeport, Alabama, whence they marched overland toward

Chattanooga. Once all these troops arrived, Bragg would be outnumbered, because he had detached Longstreet and sent him toward Knoxville, which had been occupied by Union troops under General Ambrose E. Burnside.

By late October, Union troops sallied from Chattanooga to Brown's Ferry across the Tennessee, thus opening the "Cracker Line," a new supply route into the city. Grant then planned an elaborate series of attacks to drive Bragg's troops from Chattanooga. The Battle of Chattanooga began on November 23, when units from Thomas's army left their defenses and captured Orchard Knob, giving Thomas room to maneuver.

On the 24th, troops from Hooker's command began to drive the enemy from Lookout Mountain, its peak 1,100 feet above the valley floor. Fog enshrouded much of the battle from onlookers, so that it was called "the battle above the clouds." Hooker's more numerous troops surged forward and drove the enemy from the mountain, threatening Bragg's left flank.

The major battle took place on November 25. Hooker, assigned to attack Bragg's left, was stymied by Chattanooga Creek. On the Union left, Sherman's troops assailed Bragg's right at Tunnel Hill, but the stubborn defenders under Patrick Cleburne's command repelled all of Sherman's attacks and even counterattacked, capturing some

prisoners. To relieve pressure on Sherman, Grant ordered Thomas to send four divisions forward to seize Confederate rifle pits at the base of Missionary Ridge. Once this was accomplished, however, Thomas's troops failed to heed orders to stop. Southern troops on the military crest of the ridge high above them continued to fire. Lacking orders, units began to head uphill until it appeared to Grant and Thomas, watching in horror, that the entire line was advancing. But instead of a bloody repulse, Thomas's troops surged forward and Bragg's army began to retreat in disorder.

By the end of the day, Bragg was in full retreat and Chattanooga was a major Federal victory. Losses totaled 5,815 Union soldiers and more than 6,700 Rebels, but Bragg had lost 40 cannons and his army was badly demoralized. That winter, President Davis replaced Bragg with General Joseph E. Johnston in an effort to restore the army's shaken morale.

Louis Prang lithograph showing generals Grant and Thomas watching the assault on Missionary Ridge

CHICKAMAUGA: THE RIVER OF DEATH

Cherokee Indians named this northern Georgia creek the "River of Death" because of the many intertribal battles along the stream. The blood-bath there in September 1863 only added to its meaning. And like many other scenes of combat, Chickamauga has its share of haunted tales. Veterans of the 125th Ohio erected a monument surmounted by a carved tiger, in honor of the regiment's nickname, "Opdycke's Tigers." Witnesses maintain that they have seen an other-wordly tiger prowling the battlefield at night, supposedly searching for its emerald eyes; others have been frightened by eerie green eyes staring at them through the darkness. Modern-day reenactors have encountered ghostly men from both armies, still fighting the battle over a century later.

Death at Chickamauga did not end with the Civil War. When war with Spain erupted in 1898, the government established a training camp on the battlefield. Named Camp Thomas, it was the assembly point for two army corps and associated troops, about 60,000 men in all. Lack of rail transportation meant that supplies were frequently delayed, and the troops suffered accordingly. Improper sites for camps, lack of strict discipline over the use of latrines, and close confinement of thousands of men led to a wave of typhoid fever, killing 425 men, hospitalizing thousands, and leading to a government inquiry into the problems at Camp Thomas.

General Sherman watches the Battle of Kennesaw Mountain as his frontal assault on the entrenched positions of the Confederates is repulsed with heavy losses, in what became a costly Union defeat.

KENNESAW
ON THE ROAD TO ATLANTA

The Kennesaw Mountain battlefield in Georgia is the lone park memorial to men in blue and gray who contended with each other over the fate of Atlanta in 1864. This pivotal campaign began in May 1864 and ended with the Union capture of Atlanta on September 2. Major General William T. Sherman's success in this campaign helped ensure that Abraham Lincoln would win the presidential election of 1864, and by doing so, it ensured that the Union would pursue final victory in the Civil War.

Part of the overall Union strategy for 1864 involved General Sherman's "army group," based in the Chattanooga area. Sherman, in charge of all departments from the Mississippi to the Appalachians, had three armies under his command; together, they added up to more than 110,000 soldiers. Largest was Major General George H. Thomas's Army of the Cumberland, composed of three infantry and one cavalry corps.

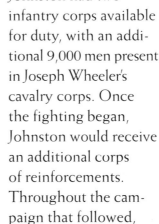

Entrenchments at Kennesaw Mountain, Georgia

Also present was much of the Army of the Tennessee, now led by Major General James B. McPherson, who had two corps on hand and another en route. Finally, Major General John M. Schofield assembled 13,000 men of the Army of the Ohio, essentially a reinforced infantry corps.

Opposed to Sherman was General Joseph E. Johnston and his 40,000-man Army of Tennessee. Johnston had two infantry corps available for duty, with an additional 9,000 men present in Joseph Wheeler's cavalry corps. Once the fighting began, Johnston would receive an additional corps of reinforcements. Throughout the campaign that followed, Johnston was tasked with preventing Sherman from penetrating deep into Southern territory, and also with covering Atlanta.

Sherman began the campaign by maneuvering Johnston out of his strong natural position at Dalton and Rocky Face Ridge. Johnston's smaller army had to fall back when its supply line was threatened, but

General Joseph E. Johnston

HUMANITY IN THE MIDST OF BATTLE

During the desperate Federal assault on June 27, gunfire ignited dry brush on the mountainside, starting several brushfires that threatened the wounded Union soldiers lying helpless near the flames. About half-an-hour after one charge, recalled Captain Robert D. Smith of the 2nd Tennessee, Confederates stopped firing and called to their enemy to come and rescue their wounded comrades. The firing stopped as the Rebels watched their enemies gather up the wounded and return to their lines. Such scenes happened on many a battlefield during the war, when nature threatened man's inhumanity to man. The bloodletting stopped long enough for the boys in blue and gray to save their comrades from burning to death.

"The sun beaming down on our uncovered heads, the thermometer being one hundred and ten degrees in the shade, and a solid line of blazing fire right from the muzzles of the Yankee guns being poured right into our very faces . . . ."

—Private Samuel R. Watkins, 1st Tennessee CSA

delay by General McPherson robbed Sherman of the opportunity to completely isolate Johnston's army. The result was a two-day battle at the railroad town of Resaca, Georgia, on May 14–15; the two armies suffered a combined loss of 7,000 men. Johnston was again forced to retreat when elements of the Union army moved south, threatening Johnston's rear lines.

During his retreat, Johnston divided his army, hoping to prod Sherman into doing the same. Then, the Confederates would quickly reunite on familiar ground and defeat a portion of Sherman's larger army. But as Johnston

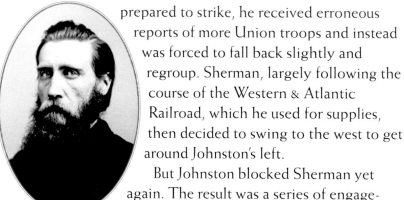

General John B. Hood

prepared to strike, he received erroneous reports of more Union troops and instead was forced to fall back slightly and regroup. Sherman, largely following the course of the Western & Atlantic Railroad, which he used for supplies, then decided to swing to the west to get around Johnston's left.

But Johnston blocked Sherman yet again. The result was a series of engagements from May 25 to June 4, known as Dallas, New Hope Church, and Pickett's Mill. Skirmishers of both armies aptly named one site the "Hell Hole." Neither side gained an advantage; Sherman then decided to move east toward the railroad again.

When Sherman began moving east, Johnston fell back to a range of mountains that protected his supply base at Marietta. Ten days of rain hampered military movements, but on June 10, Sherman again moved forward. Johnston fell back yet again to an even stronger and more compact position on Kennesaw Mountain. Four more days of rain slowed Sherman's pursuit as his army moved into position opposite the Rebels.

Sherman sent Joseph Hooker's Twentieth Corps from Thomas's army to the Union right to out-flank the Kennesaw position, but in the June 22 Battle of Kolb's Farm, Confederates from John B. Hood's corps blunted the Union attack. Then, Schofield's men went into position on Hooker's right, but found more Rebels to their front.

Wounded being removed from the battle in a sketch of combat action

Kurz & Allison lithograph depicting the Battle of Kennesaw Mountain

more than 3,000 men while Johnston reported a loss of about 1,000.

Sherman then resorted to another flanking maneuver and Johnston fell back across the Chattahoochie River, the last major barrier before Atlanta. But Johnston was unable to prevent Union troops from crossing, and after Johnston fell back to Atlanta's defenses, President Davis replaced him with Hood, a twice-wounded general known for his aggressiveness. Hood immediately sallied forth, but in a series of three battles around Atlanta—Peach Tree Creek (July 20), Atlanta (July 22), and Ezra Church (July 28)—his army suffered a total of 18,000 casualties.

After these three battles, Sherman erected siege earthworks and sent his cavalry to disrupt southern supply lines. But when his cavalry failed miserably in these raids, Sherman moved south with most of his army, cutting off the railroad at Jonesboro, south of Atlanta. After two days of fighting at Jonesboro (August 31–September 1), Hood evacuated Atlanta, burning all supplies his men could not take with them. Sherman's army entered Atlanta on September 2 as Hood withdrew to Lovejoy's Station. After Hood moved north in an attempt to interdict Sherman's supply line, Sherman divided his army, sending Thomas to confront Hood's invasion of Tennessee while he took 60,000 men and marched across Georgia to the sea.

Reports of these defenses prompted Sherman to try a frontal assault on the steep mountain. Sherman believed that Johnston might have weakened his seemingly impregnable position in order to confront the Union left, and a direct attack of his own might succeed.

Sherman readied two assault columns from Thomas's and McPherson's commands, keeping ample reserves on hand to exploit any break-through. But the Battle of Kennesaw Mountain on June 27 was a complete failure. Neither Union column made any headway. And even though elements of the attacking regiments actually reached the Confederate fortifications and engaged in hand-to-hand combat, the Rebel defenders of Patrick Cleburne's and Benjamin F. Cheatham's divisions held firm and repelled the desperate assaults. Even so, some of the attacking units dug in only yards in front of the Rebels; constant sniping over the next six days wore both sides down. Sherman's army lost

THE CIVIL WAR

COLONEL DAN McCOOK

One of the Federal brigades assaulting Kennesaw was led by Colonel Daniel McCook, a member of Ohio's "Fighting McCooks." Two McCook families sent 17 men into the Union army; their ranks ranged from private to chaplain to general.

Daniel McCook was born in 1834 and was a former law partner of William T. Sherman. McCook served in a Kansas regiment at Wilson's Creek and was later promoted to colonel of the 52nd Ohio. Sherman himself personally selected his old law partner's brigade to lead the assault on Kennesaw. Knowing the rough odds against success, Colonel McCook gave his men a pep talk by reciting the verses of "Horatius' Speech," a popular poem by British poet Thomas Macaulay.

The sad story of McCook's assault was one repeated all too often during the war. Attacking the Confederate strong point known as the Dead Angle in a desperate uphill battle, the Ohioans suffered heavy losses—more than 135 casualties, about 35 percent of the unit's strength. The Yankees reached the Rebel works and engaged in bloody hand-to-hand combat. "Colonel Dan" mounted the enemy breastwork and called for the colors to be forwarded. He was shot in the chest and collapsed. McCook died on July 17, having been promoted to brigadier general the previous day.

AMERICA'S BATTLEGROUNDS

General John B. Gordon

MONOCACY

THE BATTLE THAT SAVED WASHINGTON

In June 1864, General David Hunter's Union army advanced to Lynchburg, Virginia, before retreating across the mountains into West Virginia, where General Lee had sent an entire corps of his army to confront the Yankees. Led by General Jubal A. Early, southern troops then cleared the Shenandoah Valley of Union soldiers.

Early then chose to move his army across the Potomac into Maryland. As his army gathered supplies and ripped up the tracks of the Baltimore & Ohio Railroad, Early decided to head for Washington and threaten the city, seeking to draw off troops from Grant's army at Petersburg. To oppose the enemy advance, General Lew Wallace gathered about 3,000 men and deployed them along the east bank of the Monocacy River at Monocacy Junction, where the railroad tracks split toward Harper's Ferry and Frederick. On July 8, General James B. Ricketts's division of the Sixth Corps arrived from Petersburg, boosting Wallace's strength. The rest of the corps was still en route, detached by Grant in case they were needed.

Early's skirmishers probed the Union positions along the Monocacy on July 9. Southern horsemen located a ford beyond the Union left flank, and Early sent John B. Gordon's infantry division to secure the crossing as other units cautiously edged forward farther north. Wallace deployed Ricketts's men to face Gordon, but the more numerous southerners lapped around his flanks and Ricketts had to withdraw. Wallace pulled back the rest of his units as southern troops threatened to cross at two other bridges. The Yankees retreated toward Baltimore to protect that city from Confederate attack. Wallace had suffered more than 1,880 casualties; Early lost about 800 men.

But Wallace had delayed the Confederates by a day. When Early's men began to probe the Washington defenses on July 11, the rest of the Sixth Corps arrived to bolster the defenders. President Lincoln himself came under fire at Fort Stevens while he watched Union skirmishers in battle. Early became persuaded that he could not capture the city and thus withdrew.

It was at Fort Stevens that Early's men probed Washington's defenses. While Abraham Lincoln observed the situation in person, he came under hostile gunfire. Captain Oliver Wendell Holmes, Jr., a future Supreme Court justice, did not recognize the president and yelled at him to get down.

Federal soldiers removing artillery from Confederate fortification at the battle of Petersburg, Virginia, April 1865

PETERSBURG

THE KEY TO RICHMOND

VISITOR INFORMATION

Name Petersburg

Classification National Battlefield

Established Park—July 3, 1926. Transferred from War Department August 10, 1933; redesignated August 24, 1962. Boundary changes: June 5, 1942; September 7, 1949; August 24, 1962; April 11, 1972; November 10, 1978; December 26, 1990. Cemetery—Civil War interments: 1866. Transferred from War Department August 10, 1933

Contact 1539 Hickory Hill Road, Petersburg, VA 23803

Phone 804-732-3531

Website www.nps.gov/pete

Acreage Park—2,659.19 (Federal: 2,653.43; Nonfederal: 5.76). Cemetery—8.72 (all Federal)

Points of Focus City Point, Confederate Battery 5, Confederate Battery 8, Confederate Battery 9, The Crater, Five Forks, Fort Conahey, Fort Fisher, Fort Gregg, Fort Haskell, Fort Sedgwick, Fort Stedman, Fort Wadsworth, Poplar Grove National Cemetery, Taylor Farm

Tours/Paths 26 miles of self-guided driving tours, various walking trails

Hours Open daily from 9:00 A.M. to 5:00 P.M. Closed Thanksgiving Day, December 25, and January 1

Park Fee $3 per person or $5 per vehicle; $15 per individual annual pass

Programs Ranger-led talks, Junior Ranger program, Living History programs (summer season only)

Facilities Two visitor centers, museum, bookstore

After suffering a repulse at Cold Harbor, General Grant decided to cross the James River and attack the railroad hub of Petersburg, 23 miles south of Richmond. Grant directed General Meade, in command of the Army of the Potomac, to send most of his troops across the James, leaving a single corps, General Warren's Fifth, to mask the change of position. In the meantime, Grant ordered General Benjamin F. Butler, whose Army of the James was entrenched at Bermuda Hundred, to also send troops to attack Petersburg. If the attacks could capture the city before Lee could reinforce its defenders, Grant was sure Lee would have to abandon Richmond.

But Grant's plan went awry almost from the beginning, even though Meade directed an effective withdrawal in front of Lee's army that completely took the great southern leader by surprise. The hot June weather, exacerbated by a lack of rain, coupled with the severe loss of so many Union officers and men since the campaign had begun in May, stymied the

General Ulysses S. Grant

Army of the Potomac. Troops from Butler's army began to attack the outer defenses of Petersburg on June 15, chasing back the city's comparatively few defenders. The assaulting troops included a division of black soldiers, who gleefully took prisoners and weapons at some of the enemy fortifications.

But a lack of effective orders spelled doom for the Yankees. Fearing a trap because the early attacks encountered so few defenders, Union commanders remained cautious; by the time more troops were present, Lee had guessed where Grant was heading and was shifting his army hurriedly into Petersburg's defenses. The Union attacks sputtered to a halt on June 18. Grant's men had suffered 11,000 casualties, and even though they occupied many Confederate earthworks, Rebels had already built even more formidable lines closer to the city.

So Grant decided to initiate siege operations. Union troops began digging trenches, laying out earthwork forts, and placing abatis in front of their works to discourage attacks from the Rebels.

THE CIVIL WAR

BOLTON'S BULLET

William J. Bolton (1833–1906) served in the 51st Pennsylvania from 1861–1865, first as a captain of Company A, then as a major, and finally as colonel. He was twice wounded: at Antietam, a bullet passed through his face; in the Crater at Petersburg, Bolton was hit yet again in the same spot, but the bullet lodged in his throat. Doctors were unable to locate and remove the object. Seventeen years later, in 1881, during a fit of coughing, the bullet was dislodged and plopped into the colonel's hand. He kept it as a souvenir of his wartime service.

Colonel William J. Bolton

Union military engineers built a railroad right-of-way behind the lines to ensure a steady delivery of supplies from the base at City Point on the James River. From mid-June until April 1865, Union and Confederate soldiers remained locked in a deadly game of hide-and-seek as both sides erected formidable earthworks to deflect attacks from the other.

Grant's strategy during the siege was to keep lengthening the Union lines to make Lee match his moves, steadily weakening the enemy and forcing him to fight for control of the railroads that brought supplies from the South into Petersburg and Richmond. The first battle took place on June 22–23, as units from two Federal corps moved against the Weldon Railroad but were repulsed when Confederate troops found and exploited a gap in their lines.

Federal soldiers in the 48th Pennsylvania regiment, a unit that included a number of coal miners, convinced their colonel that they could dig a tunnel under the Confederate fortifications, pack it with gunpowder, and blow a hole in the enemy line. General Ambrose E. Burnside, their immediate corps commander, enthusiastically supported the plan, but professional engineers at army headquarters pooh-poohed the idea. Still, the men of the 48th started construction of a tunnel, using ingenuity and brawn to complete the project. Its main shaft was 511 feet in length. Burnside gathered his corps and was promised support from the rest of the army. He planned to use a black division as a spearhead for the assault, but was overruled and told to use his

white troops. Burnside had his division commanders draw straws, and as it happened the general with the least experience got the short straw. As a result, even though the explosion of the mine on July 30 was a spectacular success, Burnside's troops bungled the attack. While initially successful, it was contained by Confederate reinforcements, and the Yankees were forced to retreat. This battle, known both as the Crater and the Mine Explosion, cost Grant 5,000 casualties.

In order to divert Federal troops from Petersburg General Lee sent one of his corps into the Shenandoah Valley to reinforce its outnumbered defenders. Then, after General Jubal Early's troops had driven the Yankees out of the Valley, Early launched a raid across the Potomac River into Maryland. His troops approached the Washington fortifications but were too weak to seize the city, because troops from Grant's army arrived to bolster its defenses. The resulting Shenandoah Valley campaign ended with a complete Confederate defeat in October.

In the meantime, Lee and Grant sparred at Petersburg. Between August 18–21, troops from Warren's Fifth Corps led an advance to the Weldon Railroad. Although his men suffered heavier losses than the Confederate defenders, Warren managed to erect fortifications and held on to his territorial gain, severing the rail line at Globe Tavern.

Another Union expedition took place in late September, when troops from two corps moved west to divert attention from Butler's planned attack on Richmond. Fighting took place

Federal supplies deposited on the landing at City Point, Virginia

The Fall of Petersburg, April 2, 1865

from September 30 to October 2, but the Union expeditions only lengthened the lines without making appreciable gains. Another combat occurred on October 27, when southern defenders repelled Union attacks along the Boydton Plank Road.

After winter brought an end to active operations, Grant's troops struck in February 1865 at Hatcher's Run, but were again deflected from the Southside Railroad. But by now Lee's men were beginning to desert, and he feared that the overwhelming number of Union troops would crush his troops when spring weather dried the roads. So on March 25, General John B. Gordon's men assailed the Union siege lines, capturing Fort Stedman in a desperate bid to break through.

Union reinforcements drove Gordon's men back. Reacting to this victory, Grant sent his cavalry commander, Philip Sheridan, supported by Warren's corps, west to the White Oak Road. On March 31–April 1, Sheridan won a decisive victory, crushing George Pickett's troops at Five Forks and sealing the fate of Petersburg.

Sheridan's victory meant that the railroads were now vulnerable. On April 2, Grant ordered an attack on Petersburg's fortifications. Troops from the Sixth Corps scored a decisive breakthrough, forcing Lee to abandon his lines and retreat. Richmond, now left vulnerable, also was abandoned and occupied by Union troops on April 3. Appomattox was now less than a week away.

THEY SAID IT COULDN'T BE DONE

Once the siege lines stabilized at Petersburg in June 1864, Colonel Henry Pleasants of the 48th Pennsylvania received permission to dig a tunnel under a Confederate fort. General Meade and professional engineers at army headquarters scoffed at the idea, but corps commander Burnside approved. Starting 100 feet behind the Union front line on June 25, the 48th, which included more than 100 coal miners, began a tunnel that eventually reached 511 feet in length, then dug two lateral galleries, each about 40 feet in length, that would hold the powder to blow up the enemy fort. Working with improvised picks and having to scrounge for wood for tunnel supports, the troops completed the tunnel and its two laterals by July 23. Then, after packing 4 tons of gunpowder contained in sacks, the miners carried in more than 1,000 cubic feet of tamping to ensure that the force of the explosion would go up rather than down the tunnel. Pleasants's men had surpassed themselves with this Yankee ingenuity.

The entrance to the Union tunnel

VISITOR INFORMATION

Name Appomattox Court House

Classification National Historical Park

Established June 18, 1930. Transferred from War Department August 10, 1933; redesignated August 13, 1935; April 15, 1954. Boundary changes: February 23, 1939; October 21, 1976; December 3, 1980; October 27, 1992

Contact Highway 24, P.O. Box 218, Appomattox, VA 24522

Phone 434-352-8987, ext. 26

Website www.nps.gov/apco

Acreage 1,774.74 (Federal: 1,679.80; Nonfederal: 94.94)

Points of Focus Appomattox County Jail, Appomattox Court House, Clover Hill Tavern, Mariah Wright House, McLean House, Meeks' Store, Tavern Guest House, Woodson Law Office

Tours/Paths Self-guided walking tours, 6-mile History Trail, McLean House tours

Hours Open daily from 8:30 A.M. to 5:00 P.M. Closed Thanksgiving Day, December 25, and January 1

Park Fee From Memorial Day to Labor Day: $4 per person, maximum $10 per vehicle; from Labor Day to Memorial Day: $3 per person, maximum $5 per vehicle. Ages 16 and under free

Programs Two 15-minute audio visual presentations, Living History programs (summer season only)

Facilities Visitor center, museum, bookstore, picnic areas

General Ulysses S. Grant

APPOMATTOX

END OF THE WAR

Union troops breached the Confederate defenses of Petersburg on April 2, 1865. General Lee then decided to abandon Petersburg and Richmond, move west about 40 miles to Amelia Court House to gather supplies, then turn south in an attempt to unite with General Joseph E. Johnston's southern army in North Carolina. Then, Lee thought, their combined strength could defeat General William T. Sherman's army before Grant and Sherman united.

But when Lee arrived at Amelia Court House, he found no supplies as anticipated. Worse, Grant kept up a close pursuit in an effort to prevent Lee from moving south. On April 6 General Sheridan's Yankees caught up with the Confederate rearguard at Saylor's Creek. Union assaults overwhelmed the outnumbered defenders, 7,000 of whom surrendered, effectively destroying Lee's Second Corps.

Lee continued his retreat as his army melted away. Food was scarce and many soldiers, realizing that their cause was doomed, began to desert. But many

The reconstructed McLean House

thousands remained loyal to their great chief and marched onward even as Union troops, marching along parallel roads to the south, maneuvered into position in front of Lee's men. Lee hesitated to attack, then sent a message to Grant, asking for terms of surrender. Lee realized that his outnumbered army was virtually surrounded, short on supplies and ammunition, and in danger of annihilation.

Lee and Grant met in Wilmer McLean's house in the tiny village of Appomattox Court House. After some discussion, Lee agreed to Grant's generous terms. His men would all be paroled as prisoners of war and sent home. Men who owned horses would be allowed to take them along to help with spring planting. Officers would retain their swords, but all firearms, flags, and cannon would be surrendered. The official surrender ceremony took place on April 12, when approximately 28,000 Confederate soldiers laid down their arms and went home. Other Confederate armies followed suit and by mid-May, most southern troops had given up the struggle and the Civil War was over.

Capitulation and surrender of Robert E. Lee and his army to General U.S. Grant at Appomattox, Virginia, on April 9, 1865

This grave of an American soldier killed in the 1945 invasion of Normandy, France, is marked "Died For France."

MEMORIALS TO COURAGE

1942–1976

With the closure of the frontier in 1890, American expansion across the continent was complete. The nation had largely grown past the pains of the late Civil War, and expansionists were advocating an overseas empire to satiate the growing nation. War with Spain in 1898 fueled America's ambitions. In a conflict that lasted only 100 days, the burgeoning military power of the United States defeated the faltering Spanish Empire. By the terms of the peace treaty, America acquired the Philippines, Guam, Puerto Rico, and Cuba. But this brief war spawned no overseas memorials; only state and local monuments, together with

gas mask tin

THE USS *MAINE*

The remains of the battleship *Maine* lay in Havana harbor until 1911, when the U. S. Navy built a cofferdam around the ship, recovered some human remains, and convened a study to examine the cause of the ship's demise. In 1912, the study complete, the rear two-thirds of the *Maine* were refloated, towed to sea, and sunk in deeper water.

In 1913, a memorial dedicated to the ship and its 264 dead was opened in Arlington National Cemetery. This memorial features the ship's main mast atop a stylized turret base. During the ensuing years, the Navy Department distributed hundreds of relics from the *Maine* to communities and veterans' organizations across the nation. Today, many of these relics can be seen in museums and historical societies. Even pieces of iron plate were salvaged, cut into rectangles, and engraved with the name of the ill-fated ship.

"The first time you kill a man is one feeling. The first time you look him straight in the face and shoot him and kill him, that's another feeling, and after that it doesn't make much difference."

—Charles Meacham, 3rd Raider Battalion, 4th Marine Regiment, 1st Provisional Brigade

salvaged pieces of the ill-fated battleship *Maine*, served to remind Americans of this brief struggle.

When the First World War erupted in Europe in 1914, the United States, led by President Woodrow Wilson, tried hard to remain neutral. But German U-boat operations and other incitements turned public opinion against the Germans and eased the declaration of war that America made against Germany in 1917. The arrival of thousands of American troops, under the command of General John J. Pershing, enabled the Allies to blunt the German offensive of 1918 and force an armistice that became the end of the war.

American troops came home to tumultuous welcomes. They had made the world safe for democracy, but America remained isolationist. Congress voted against joining the new League of Nations. State governments helped create monu-

ments to their heroic troops where they fought on the Western Front; the American Battle Monuments Commission was created in 1923 to administer these memorials on foreign soil as well as cemeteries holding the remains of those who were not brought home.

New threats from Germany, Italy, and Japan developed into an international crisis and a second world war in 1939. The United States again tried to remain neutral, but President Franklin D. Roosevelt established the Lend-Lease program to help Great Britain stem the Nazi tide. As Japan turned aggressive, America began embargoing products Japan needed to wage war. Becoming more desperate as shortages developed, Japan's leaders gambled on a surprise attack on the American Pacific Fleet based in Pearl Harbor, Hawaii. As a result, after December 7, 1941,

Wreck of the USS Maine, *June 7, 1911*

America entered the war. By its end in 1945, the United States had suffered over a 1,000,000 casualties but had emerged as a major power in world affairs. This time, America was among the first to join the new United Nations organization.

This time, too, American troops remained overseas as the threat of Communist domination loomed. In June 1950, Communist troops of North Korea invaded South Korea in a bid to take over the entire divided country. The USSR representative to the United Nations was absent, which enabled the Western allies to gain authorization to counter the North Korean invasion. American troops fought in this undeclared Korean War, officially a "police action" but in reality a brutal war, from 1950 to 1953. Communist China sent troops to assist North Korea, and after a year of see-saw warfare, the last two years of the conflict saw a stalemate develop. The 1953 cease-fire resulted in today's border between the two Koreas. American casualties totaled 157,530, including 54,246 deaths.

American troops then became engaged in an escalating dispute between North and South Vietnam. The North, under Communist control, sought to annex the South, an American ally. American troops followed advisors as a rapid military

A dead American soldier on the Western Front in World War I

U.S. poster from World War II

buildup in the South during the 1960s escalated into a major conflict between America and North Vietnam, which was aided covertly by the USSR and China. The Vietnam War was easily America's most unpopular war. Anti-war unrest included riots and student protests on campuses across the country. Their protests helped undermine whatever success America had achieved on the jungle-covered battlefields in South Vietnam. This was the first conflict to appear on the nightly news in homes all over America. As a result, America withdrew from the war in 1975; shortly thereafter, a weakened South Vietnam fell to a massive invasion from the north. American losses totaled 210,988, with 57,685 dead.

As with Korea, there were no festive homecomings as America quickly tried to forget its first loss in a war. Veterans were often shunted aside and discriminated against as the nation tried to heal from years of social unrest. Again, there would be no memorials for those who survived an unpopular war. But in recent years, veterans have succeeded in focusing attention on those who were forgotten by the public at large. Monuments to heroism in Korea and Vietnam now remind Americans that their veterans have contributed mightily to the growth of the nation and the freedoms enjoyed by her people.

WAR MEMORIALS ABROAD

Memorials to American military personnel can be found in 14 foreign countries, primarily in Western Europe. In 1923, Congress formed the American Battle Monuments Commission (ABMC), which is charged with taking care of these monuments, as well as maintaining 24 cemeteries that contain the remains of about 125,000 American dead (those who fought in the Mexican War, World War I, and World War II). The ABMC has jurisdiction over 27 war memorials, including 5 memorials located in the United States. Two of these are World War II memorials in New York City and San Francisco that commemorate merchant vessel casualties. The commission also oversees the Korean War Memorial in Washington and was in charge of the construction of the World War II memorial that opened April 28, 2004. Additional monuments located in France that commemorate World War I units are the responsibility of unit organizations and state governments.

The National World War II Memorial, the newest of the ABMC's responsibilities

VISITOR INFORMATION

Name USS *Arizona*

Classification Memorial

Established May 30, 1968; redesignated September 19, 1980 (Memorial now owned by U.S. Navy and administered by the National Park Service under a cooperative agreement)

Contact 1 Arizona Memorial Place, Honolulu, HI 96818

Phone 808-422-0561

Website www.nps.gov/usar

Acreage 10.50 (all Federal)

Points of Focus The Hill of Sacrifice, Remembrance Exhibit, Shrine Room, Visitor Center

Tours/Paths Self-guided tour through memorial

Hours Open daily, 7:30 A.M. to 5:00 P.M.

Park Fee Free

Programs 23-minute film on Pearl Harbor attack, boat ride to USS *Arizona* Memorial, Junior Ranger Program for ages 7–12

Facilities Visitor center, museum, bookstore, shoreline exhibits

PEARL HARBOR

DAY OF INFAMY

December 7, 1941 was "a date that will live in infamy," to borrow a phrase from President Franklin D. Roosevelt's speech before Congress on December 8. December 7 is one of those defining moments in American history, when a surprise attack brought America into active participation in World War II.

American entry had long been coming, but FDR, bowing to isolationist tendencies in this country, had tried hard to avoid declaring war. American aid substantially helped Great Britain ward off German attacks. In the Pacific, Americans worried about Japanese expansion. Although it had been on the Allied side in World War I, Japan did not reap the same territorial benefits that other countries did, and that failure angered Japanese expansionists. By the early 1930s, Japan's government was controlled by mili-

President Roosevelt signs the declaration of war.

tarists who sought to bring the nation to power as guardian of East Asia.

Japanese expansion into China erupted into open war in 1937. America, worried about Japanese militarism, struck back by identifying an ever-increasing list of embargoed items necessary for Japan to sustain its ambitions. In May 1940, the U.S. Pacific Fleet moved to a new headquarters—Pearl Harbor, Hawaii. The Hawaiian Islands were strategically situated between the two antagonists; it was hoped that the American fleet's new location would prove a deterrent against Japanese aggression. But in September 1940, Japan, Germany, and Italy signed the Tripartite Pact, an alliance that bound these three nations together if any one of them were attacked.

Even as negotiators in Washington tried to work out smoother relations between America and Japan, Japanese officers were already planning a surprise strike at Pearl Harbor in case negotiations failed. Allied embargoes had already curtailed Japan's overseas sources of oil, threatening its ability to wage war. As a result, its military planned a series of attacks in late 1941 that would cripple American response and allow the Japanese to consolidate their hold on the western Pacific.

Sailors rescue swimming comrades as the USS *West Virginia* burns after the Japanese aerial attack on Pearl Harbor. The USS *Tennessee*'s superstructure is visible in the background. Both battleships were repaired and took part in later operations in the Pacific, generally as fire support of amphibious landings. These older battlewagons were too slow to keep up with aircraft carriers.

JAPAN BOMBS AMERICA!

The Japanese attack on Pearl Harbor was not the only Japanese assault on American soil. Japanese submarines occasionally shelled the West Coast but inflicted no civilian casualties. In 1942, as part of the Midway operation, Japanese troops landed on the Aleutian Islands in Alaska. Starting in November 1944, in a desperate attempt to bomb America, the Japanese used westerly winds to launch more than 9,000 paper balloons, each carrying a 30-pound bomb toward the United States. Although most never reached their targets, one actually landed in Maryland. On May 5, 1945, a family out on a picnic stumbled upon a bomb in the Oregon woods. It exploded and killed a woman and five children, the only civilians on the American mainland killed during World War II.

American soldiers fire mortar shells into Japanese positions on Attu Island in the Aleutians in 1943.

On November 26, 1941, a Japanese armada under the command of Admiral Chiuchi Nagumo steamed out of the Kurile Islands, bound for the seas north of Hawaii. Under strict radio silence, the fleet approached Hawaii. Even though America had broken Japan's secret diplomatic codes, it was uncertain where Japan's fleet was headed. Back in 1932, during a war-game exercise, an American admiral had launched carrier aircraft that surprised Pearl Harbor and demonstrated the effectiveness of naval airpower. But in 1941 many old salts yet believed that the battleship was still the queen of the seas. The American Pacific Fleet had eight such behemoths, and all were at their docks in Pearl Harbor on December 7. The fleet's three aircraft carriers were all absent on other missions.

Once it was known in Tokyo that negotiations in Washington were deadlocked, approval was given to attack Pearl Harbor. Aircraft from six carriers—fighters, torpedo bombers, and dive bombers—planned to strike Pearl Harbor at dawn on Sunday, December 7. Meanwhile Japanese ambassadors in Washington were instructed to deliver an ultimatum to the American government at one o'clock that afternoon—7:00 A.M. in Hawaii. But they were delayed half-an-hour while waiting for a message from Tokyo, and by the time the message was received at the State Department, bombs had already fallen on Hawaii.

The first Japanese planes struck at 7:51 A.M. Targets included all the air bases on Hawaii, to ensure that the planes attacking the American fleet would not be opposed. Fearing sabotage, many American planes were parked wingtip to wingtip so that the guards would be better able to watch them. As a result, they were sitting ducks for strafing and bombing by Japanese planes. In spite of the odds against them, some American

pilots managed to get airborne and were able to engage their opponents in air combat.

Meanwhile, Pearl Harbor itself turned into an inferno. The moored ships were easy targets for the torpedo and dive bombers that swarmed over the anchorage. Six of the fleet's battleships were moored off Ford Island in "Battleship Row," while the flagship *Pennsylvania* was in drydock for repairs; she escaped serious damage during the attack. The remaining battlewagon—the old *Utah*—was moored on the opposite side of Ford Island. But the other battleships were not so lucky. The *West Virginia* and *California* were hit by torpedoes and settled upright onto the harbor bottom. The *Tennessee* and *Maryland* managed to escape with only bomb damage. The *Oklahoma* was hit by six torpedoes and rolled over, settling at a 30-degree angle on the bottom. The *Nevada* suffered some damage, but her skipper managed to get up enough steam so that by the time the second enemy wave arrived, the great ship was heading for the harbor mouth. But the *Nevada* attracted lots of attention, and to prevent her from sinking and blocking the harbor, her captain grounded the stricken vessel.

At 8:06, an armor-piercing bomb dropped onto the *Arizona* and struck the forward magazine. A survivor remembered that "the entire ship shuddered." A mammoth fireball erupted 500 feet into the air, blowing men off the decks of nearby ships. Hundreds died instantly, including her captain and an admiral. When the survivors were counted, 1,177 were declared dead or missing. Launched in 1915, the *Arizona*, like her sister ships, mounted twelve 14-inch guns and twenty-two 5-inch secondary guns.

Of the active battleships attacked that day, only the *Arizona* and *Oklahoma* were total losses. All others were repaired and modernized and fought throughout the war. The *Utah*, which had

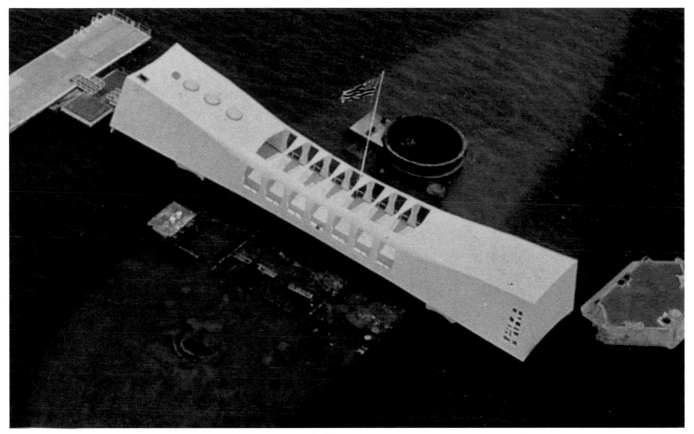

The USS Arizona Memorial at Pearl Harbor spans the sunken hull of the battleship and commemorates the American servicemen killed in the attack that catapulted the United States into World War II.

WWII AVIATION

The attack on Pearl Harbor demonstrated the devastating effects of the airpower that revolutionized modern warfare. Tens of thousands of planes took part in World War II, including reconnaissance aircraft, medical craft, bombers, fighters, and other specialized craft. Many veteran aircraft of the 1940s have been preserved by individuals, groups, and museums. Hundreds of surviving planes can be seen across America in various museums and at air shows. The National Air and Space Museum in Washington, DC, and its new adjunct, the Udvar-Hazy Center at Dulles International Airport, contain World War II planes and exhibits. The United States Air Force Museum at Wright-Patterson Air Force Base, Dayton, Ohio, is perhaps the best starting place to see a host of World War II aircraft. The National Museum of Naval Aviation in Pensacola, Florida, is well worth visiting to see examples of naval warplanes.

been converted into a target ship, was also sunk and remains so to this day. In 1962, the *Arizona* officially opened as a memorial, representing all 2,395 servicemen killed at Pearl Harbor. The bulk of the wreck was salvaged, leaving only the main hull underwater. Many of her survivors are now buried in the hull, joining dead comrades asleep since 1941.

But the *Arizona* was already obsolete when she blew up. Short of battleships at first, America relied on aircraft carriers to sustain its fleet. As the navy grew in strength, carriers became the centerpieces of naval strategy and were used as the main strike forces for the counteroffensive that resulted in Japan's surrender in September 1945. Ironically,

the instrument of surrender was signed aboard the USS *Missouri*, one of America's mighty battleships. One of four ships of the Iowa class, the *Missouri* had been authorized back in 1934, but not launched until early 1944. At 45,000 tons, the *Missouri* was capable of 33 knots. Her nine 16-inch guns were equipped to lob armor-piercing shells more than 20 miles. After fighting at Iwo Jima and Okinawa, the *Missouri* witnessed the surrender ceremony in Tokyo Bay. The "Mighty Mo" saw active service off Korea and was a participant in Desert Storm in the 1990s before being retired to serve as a memorial for the Pacific War.

B-24 Liberator

Remains of many warships from confrontations during World War II can be found in the shallow waters off Micronesia. Here, tourists explore a sunken Japanese military ship, a casualty of one battle.

THE PACIFIC
ISLAND-HOPPING TOWARD JAPAN

War in the Pacific National Historical Park represents the Allied offensive that started with the landings on Guadalcanal in August 1942. By early 1944, American forces under General Douglas MacArthur had cleared the Solomon Islands of Japanese troops and were advancing in New Guinea. In the central Pacific, American naval forces covered amphibious operations in the Marshall and Gilbert island groups.

Planning then began for an invasion of the Mariana Islands—Saipan, Tinian, and Guam. Seizure of these islands would bring the new B-29 bombers within striking distance of the Japanese islands themselves. Guam had been an American possession since 1898, when an American expeditionary force en route to the Philippines seized the island. In fact, the Spanish governor didn't even know there was a war going on; when an American warship steamed into the anchorage on the west coast and fired a warning shot, the governor sent an emissary to apologize for his lack of ammunition to fire a return salute!

American carrier aircraft from Admiral Raymond Spruance's Fifth Fleet softened up the Marianas with massive air strikes, alerting the Japanese about American intentions. In response, the Imperial Japanese Navy sallied forth to attack the Americans. But U.S. submarines spotted the enemy and alerted the surface fleet as to their whereabouts. On June 15, U.S. Marines swarmed ashore on Saipan as Japanese warships steamed into range of the Americans and launched a series of aircraft strikes on the American carrier groups under the immediate command of Rear Admiral Marc Mitscher. The ill-trained Japanese pilots were shot down by American fighters and a barrage of antiaircraft fire from the ships. In the two-day Battle of the Philippine Sea (June 19–20), almost 400 Japanese planes were downed, compared to a loss of 23 American planes. The great "Marianas Turkey Shoot" destroyed Japan's remaining naval aircraft strength; the Japanese also lost three carriers.

On Saipan, Marines drove the enemy northward and ended all effective resistance by July 9. On July 21, after an intensive naval and air bombardment, the 3rd Marine Division and 1st Marine Brigade

A U.S. Navy Avenger torpedo bomber takes part in attacks on Tinian Island in the Marianas in 1944, after the fortunes of war had shifted decisively in favor of the Americans.

VISITOR INFORMATION

Name War in the Pacific

Classification National Historical Park

Established August 18, 1978

Contact 460 North Marine Drive, Maintenance Facility, Piti, GU 96915

Phone 671-472-7240

Website www.nps.gov/wapa

Acreage 1,992.28 (Federal: 919.33; Nonfederal: 1,072.05 Water area: 1,002.00)

Points of Focus Apaca Point, Asan Bay Overlook, Asan Beach Park, Ga'an Point, Piti Guns Unit

Tours/Paths Hiking trails

Hours Open daily from 8:00 A.M. to 3:00 P.M. Closed Thanksgiving Day, December 25, and January 1

Park Fee Free

Programs Kayaking, snorkeling, and swimming at Asan Beach Park

Note The super-typhoon Pongsona struck on December 8, 2002, and caused extensive damage to this park. Programs and facilities are slowly being reintroduced. For specific information, contact the park before you arrive.

THE LAST JAPANESE SOLDIER

Once Guam was secured by American troops in 1944, the island was turned into a giant airbase. After the war was over, life got back to normal—for most people. Occasional Japanese soldiers continued to turn up years after the fighting ended. Isolated from their comrades, these survivors remained hidden, stealing from civilians and living in the jungle. The last known Japanese survivor, Sergeant Shoichi Yokoi, was caught by fishermen in 1972 who found him trying to set shrimp traps. He had escaped the fighting in Guam with a few of his compatriots, all of whom died at least eight years before Yokoi was found. Yokoi had lived for almost thirty years in a cave hidden behind a waterfall, making his own clothes from the fibers of hibiscus plants and surviving on a diet consisting of everything from coconuts to rats. He returned to Japan as a national celebrity, and his memoir of 28 years in the jungle appeared later that same year.

Shoichi Yokoi, greeting Japanese press

landed on Guam's western beaches. The Japanese commander, General Takeshi Takashina, had decided to throw all his troops at the enemy in an attempt to prevent the Marines from gaining a foothold. Between July 25–27, Japanese troops charged the American positions, at times overrunning some and penetrating into the rear areas. But the Marines held, and the enemy was never able to mount another major offensive.

The Marines were reinforced by the 77th Infantry Division. The surviving enemy soldiers largely retreated toward the rugged terrain on the north end of Guam. This allowed the Americans to consolidate the rest of the island and mass their forces for a push northward, which began in late July. By August 10, organized resistance had ended. American casualties were 1,744 dead and 5,970 wounded. The Japanese garrison was exterminated, with about 19,500 dead and an unprecedented 1,250 captured.

As the Japanese resistance on Guam ended, surviving Chamorro people, the native civilization of the Marianas, began to enter American lines. Days before the American landing, the Japanese had begun to kill groups of islanders

so that they would not make trouble during the anticipated fighting. Some heroic men overpowered their guards and liberated their families, then fled into the jungles on the island. The survivors told their liberators of the wartime cruelty perpetrated on them by the Japanese, and of their joy at finally being liberated.

But liberation also meant a radical lifestyle change. After American troops made short work of Japanese troops on Tinian (July 24–August 1), all three islands were turned into giant airfields to accommodate B-29 squadrons that were sent to raid Japan. The lives of the islanders would be changed forever.

This old tank from World War II is now overgrown with ferns and plants in the Solomon Islands.

SUBMARINES

During World War II, the United States launched a force of 319 submarines against the Axis Powers; most of this force operated in the Pacific. American submarines sank more than 200 Japanese warships. More important, they sank 1,113 merchant vessels that totaled more than 5,000,000 tons, greatly aiding the Allied war effort. These totals might have been even greater but for the nearly useless torpedoes used by U.S. submarines early in the war. A defect in the arming mechanism of the warhead caused many perfectly aimed torpedoes to bounce harmlessly off the sides of Japanese ships. Once this was remedied in early 1943, American submarines dominated Japanese supply routes. The USS *Tautog* sank 26 vessels; the USS *Tang* was credited with 24. The cost was high—52 subs lost and 3,505 crew members dead. Submarines rescued 504 downed aviators, including future president George H. W. Bush. Today, travelers can visit 13 surviving submarines that saw combat; these memorials are located in 13 different states.

A Japanese miniature sub, captured after the sneak attack on Pearl Harbor

A B-29 Superfortress bomber on Saipan in the Mariana Islands is loaded with bombs readied by U.S. soldiers for a raid on Tokyo.

AMERICA'S BATTLEGROUNDS

KOREA

THE FORGOTTEN WAR

On June 25, 1950, troops of communist North Korea surged across the border into South Korea in a bid to overrun the South and reunite the divided country. The South, an ally of the United States, was no match for the better-equipped Communist forces. President Harry S. Truman, with United Nations support, appointed Douglas MacArthur as commanding general of the rapidly escalating U.N. presence in the South. By the time the front stabilized, U.N. forces were pushed into the Pusan perimeter in the southeastern corner of the peninsula.

MacArthur launched a daring amphibious landing at Inchon on September 15, taking the enemy by surprise and starting a northward retreat that carried U.N. forces into North Korean territory. But this advance triggered a massive Chinese intervention and forced a U.N. retreat.

By mid-1951, the front had stabilized and negotiations were begun to end the war. Chinese attacks at places such as Pork Chop Hill made headlines as the enemy argued over insignificant terrain features just to prove a point. Finally, after General Dwight D. Eisenhower won the 1952 presidential election, an armistice was signed and the war came to an end. United Nations casualties exceeded 450,000, with North Korean and Chinese losses estimated at more than 1.5 million.

Politically and militarily, the war was inconclusive. Perhaps this is why Korean War veterans came home to a less than enthusiastic reception. Few memorials were erected to honor their sacrifices. In fact, it wasn't until 1986 that a national memorial was authorized in the nation's capital. This memorial, dedicated in July 1995, features 19 stainless-steel statues that depict a typical wartime patrol and includes representatives of all American armed forces branches that served in Korea. A polished granite wall is etched with a mural showing faces taken from actual photos of Korean War soldiers. "Freedom is not free" is also etched into the granite, which reminds viewers of the trials endured by those who fought in this undeclared war.

General Dwight D. Eisenhower and General Mark W. Clark (back seat)

The Korean War Memorial features this group of 19 life-sized, stainless steel statues of soldiers of the 1950s. Created by World War II veteran Frank Gaylord, these statues vividly portray men facing the grim realities of war in a faraway country. Their wind-blown ponchos reflect the wet, miserable conditions endured by U.S. troops and those from 21 other United Nations countries.

VIETNAM

THE CONTROVERSIAL WAR

VISITOR INFORMATION

Name Vietnam Veterans

Classification Memorial

Established July 1, 1980

Contact 900 Ohio Drive, SW, Washington, DC 20024

Phone 202-426-6841

Website www.nps.gov/vive

Acreage 2.20 (all Federal)

Points of Focus Flagpole, The Three Servicemen Statue, Vietnam Women's Memorial, The Vietnam Veterans Memorial Wall

Tours/Paths Ranger-led tours

Hours Open daily from 8:00 A.M. to 11:45 P.M. Closed December 25

Park Fee Free

Programs Interpretive programs, Ranger-led discussions, Junior Ranger program

Facilities Ranger station

Without a doubt, a visit to the Vietnam Memorial on the mall in Washington, DC, is a moving experience. Completed in 1982, the V-shaped memorial was designed by Yale student Maya Ying. Its polished black granite walls contain the names of 58,209 Americans killed or presumed dead during the Vietnam War. The names are arranged in chronological order and provide a stark reminder of the cost of armed conflict. Funds for the memorial were contributed by a broad spectrum of Americans and were coordinated by a veterans' foundation established to memorialize this unpopular war. Two additions—in 1984 and 1993—of life-size bronze statues have been added to the original memorial. The veterans who envisioned a national memorial hoped that such a site would help with national healing from the scars of Vietnam.

Like Korea, Vietnam was a foreign war with no clear victory in sight. Nightly television newscasts showed the ugly side of this war. Widespread student unrest at college campuses across the nation was fueled by American incursions into Laos and Cambodia as well as by the unpopular draft. Finally, the Paris Accords, signed in January 1973, brought most American prisoners of war home as the United States ended its active involvement. South Vietnam survived only until 1975, when a massive Communist offensive smashed the South's army and toppled the government. In 1976, Vietnam was officially reunited.

For Vietnam veterans, the war's cost was staggering. Thousands of men were missing, either dead or captive, a sticking point that prevented American recognition of Vietnam for years. Many veterans came home with health problems, a result of jungle warfare, drug and alcohol abuse, and exposure to defoliants such as Agent Orange. Many had psychological problems that demanded attention. As a result of all this, Vietnam veterans were often shunted aside as an embarrassment to their country in the immediate aftermath of this costly war. But they needed healing just as much as the social rifts that afflicted America did. The establishment of a national memorial has gone a long way toward recognizing their contributions to American freedoms.

U.S. prisoners of war reporting to American representatives at the airport in Hanoi

WORLD TRADE CENTER MEMORIAL

The space where the twin towers once stood in Manhattan will be dedicated as a memorial for all those who died there. The design of the memorial was decided upon in a competition and the winning concept, "Reflecting Absence," by architects Michael Arad and Peter Walker, creates a place where Americans may grieve their losses and find meaning in the attack. The final memorial will incorporate randomly flowing water over the names of the deceased to symbolize the random brutality of the attack. The names of six people killed in the 1993 World Trade Center bombing will also be included here. Unidentified remains will be interred at the bottom of the North Tower's footprint, and a crushed fire truck as well as some of the towers' steel beams will also be displayed.

SEPTEMBER 11
TERROR ATTACK

The events of September 11, 2001, when foreign terrorists brought their hatred of the United States to the nation's own shores, graphically demonstrated that we are involved in a global conflict that begs of easy solutions. Although the attacks that day were shocking to Americans, terrorism is not a new idea. Americans have been fighting terrorism ever since 1801, when Thomas Jefferson authorized the use of force against Barbary Pirates who had been terrorizing merchant vessels along the North African coast for decades. Theodore Roosevelt dealt with the kidnapping of American citizens in Morocco, and in 1916–17 the United States sent troops into Mexico to track down Pancho Villa in the wake of his raids across the border.

The end of World War II and the collapse of colonial empires brought long-repressed strife into the open as ethnic and religious groups fought for recognition of their rights. News stories of the past two decades reveal how this strife has affected America. The United States's bombing of Libya in 1986, the destruction of Pan Am Flight 103 over Lockerbie, Scotland, in 1988, the World Trade Center bombing in 1993, and the attack on the USS *Cole* in 2000 all serve as reminders of the worldwide terrorism problem.

But the September 11 attacks truly changed America. That morning, Islamic terrorists hijacked four airplanes—two from Boston, one from Newark, New Jersey, and one from Dulles International Airport outside Washington. They crashed the two from Boston into the twin towers of the World Trade Center in New York City. The plane from Dulles blasted into the side of the Pentagon. The fourth plane crashed into a field in southern Pennsylvania after some of its passengers fought with the hijackers and foiled their mission, which apparently was to crash into the White House.

The attacks left 2,749 Americans dead and changed the lives of ordinary Americans far more than any recent event. The attacks led to American military operations in Afghanistan, resulting in the deaths of American military personnel, who became the latest casualties in a long list of military operations in defense of American freedoms. The terrorist attacks and their aftermath attest to the saying, "Freedom is not free."

A portion of the southwest E Ring of the Pentagon was struck by one of the hijacked planes.

The south tower, left, of the World Trade Center is rocked by a fiery explosion as United Airlines flight 175 crashes into it. The north tower is already in flames from an earlier attack. While the towers remained standing long enough to allow thousands to escape, their eventual collapse buried hundreds of firefighters and policemen who had come to rescue those trapped in the upper floors.

INDEX

INDEX

CREDITS

AMERICA'S BATTLEGROUNDS

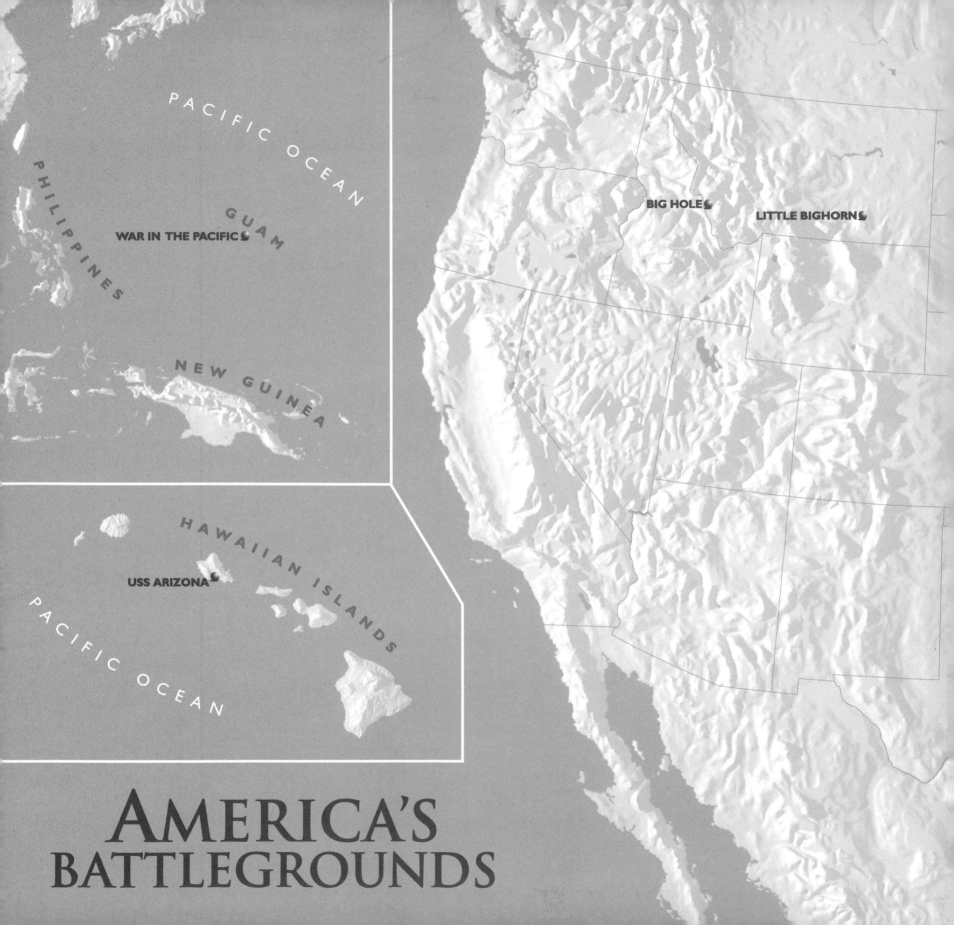

PACIFIC OCEAN

PHILIPPINES

GUAM

WAR IN THE PACIFIC

NEW GUINEA

HAWAIIAN ISLANDS

USS ARIZONA

PACIFIC OCEAN

BIG HOLE

LITTLE BIGHORN

AMERICA'S BATTLEGROUNDS